Aging and Communication: Problems in Management

The *Advanced Models and Practice in Aged Care* series:

Number 1

The Acting-Out Elderly edited by Miriam K. Aronson, Ruth Bennett, and Barry J. Gurland

Number 2

Coordinated Service Delivery Systems for the Elderly: New Approaches for Care & Referral in New York State edited by Ruth Bennett, Susana Frisch, Barry Gurland, and David Wilder

Number 3

Aging and Communication: Problems in Management edited by Carol N. Wilder and Barbara E. Weinstein

Series Editors: Ruth Bennett, PhD, and Barry J. Gurland, MD, MRCP

Advanced Models and Practice in Aged Care
Number 3

Aging and Communication: Problems in Management

Edited by

Carol N. Wilder, PhD
Barbara E. Weinstein, PhD

Teachers College
Columbia University

The Haworth Press
New York

RC
423
.A345
1984

105478

The Haworth Press, Inc., 28 East 22 Street, New York, NY 10010

Library of Congress Cataloging in Publication Data
Main entry under title:

Aging and communication.

(Advanced models and practice in aged care ; no. 3)
Includes bibliographical references.
1. Communicative disorders—Treatment. 2. Aged—Diseases. I. Wilder, Carol N.
II. Weinstein, Barbara E. III. Series. [DNLM: 1. Hearing disorders—In old age—Congresses. 2. Language disorders—In old age—Congresses. 3. Speech disorders—In old age—Congresses. 4. Health services for the aged—Congresses. WM 475 A2665 1981]
RC423.A345   1984   618.97'6855   83-26545
ISBN 0-86656-156-0

CONTENTS

Dedicated to

Ira M. Ventry, Ph.D.

Foreword

On October 18, 1981, Columbia University's Department of Speech and Language Pathology and Audiology at Teachers College in co-sponsorship with the Brookdale Institute on Aging and Adult Human Development presented a one day conference entitled "Aging and Communication: Problems and Management." It was organized with the cooperation of the Long Term Care Gerontology Center of the Center for Geriatrics and Gerontology, Columbia University Faculty of Medicine.

The conference program was the first of its kind at Columbia and one of only a handful of such programs anywhere that had been organized to seriously consider in systematic fashion the communication disorders associated with old age. It had as its primary purpose to sensitize a multidisciplinary group of community professionals—occupational and physical therapists, nurses, social workers, nursing home administrators, directors of senior citizen centers, agency administrators, and others—to the prevalence of communication disorders, the diagnosis of speech, hearing and language problems, and most importantly, how best to provide services to those in need of remedial help. To accomplish this purpose, the conference program was organized around two themes: (1) a description of communication processes and problems in the elderly, and (2) the specification of current management techniques and approaches to the delivery of related services. A distinguished faculty was drawn together for this event to address such topics as language and aging, environmental influences on communication, approaches to diagnosis and rehabilitation, and legislation affecting the provision of services.

The edited proceedings contained herein reflect the timeliness and quality of the presentations and subsequent discussion that took place during that meeting. It serves to document the complexity and pervasiveness of gerontologic communication disorders and the formidable obstacles such conditions can come to represent in the total care of the impaired elderly residing in both institutional and noninstitutional settings. A wide range of allied health and social welfare professionals as well as students in training should find this volume to be an exceedingly important resource in their daily clinical work with the elderly.

Abraham Monk, PhD
Brookdale Professor of Gerontology
School of Social Work
Director
Brookdale Institute on Aging
and Adult Human Development
Columbia University

Lenard W. Kaye, DSW
Research Scientist
School of Social Work
Associate Director
Brookdale Institute on Aging
and Adult Human Development
Columbia University

Aging and Communication: Problems in Management

Introduction

Speech, language, and hearing disorders occur more frequently in older adults than in any other age group. Thus, these disorders present a pervasive problem, not only for the elderly, but also for the professionals who provide services for them. If unrecognized or untreated, a communication disorder can have a profound impact on the quality of an individual's life and can serve as a formidable obstacle to the total management of the elderly. Although speech-language pathologists and audiologists have primary responsibility for the identification and treatment of communication impairments, the understanding and assistance of the other professionals concerned with this population is essential for the provision of optimal services.

Health professionals working with the elderly acknowledge that their training does not provide an adequate understanding of normal and/or disordered communication. In recognition of their need for knowledge in this area, a conference titled "Aging and Communication: Problems and Management" was mounted by the Department of Speech-Language Pathology and Audiology at Teachers College, Columbia University and the Brookdale Institute on Aging and Adult Human Development, Columbia University, with the cooperation of the Center for Geriatrics and Gerontology, Faculty of Medicine, Columbia University. Information was presented regarding the prevalence of communication disorders, the diagnosis of speech, language, and hearing problems, and most importantly, how best to provide services to those in need of remedial help. This monograph is a compilation of the papers presented at that conference, and is organized in the same way, with an overview of communication problems in the elderly followed by a discussion of management techniques and delivery systems. These papers are not intended as in-depth reviews of the topics; rather, their purpose is to sensitize concerned professionals to the scope and impact of communication impairments in the elderly, and to the role of the speech-language pathologist and audiologist in the provision of comprehensive services for this population.

BW
CW

Speech and Language Pathology and Audiology: An Overview

Edward D. Mysak

My specific task in this most interesting conference on aging and communication is to provide a brief overview of the field of speech and language pathology and audiology and its concern for aging of communicative processes. I will also report on some of the activities of the Department of Speech and Language Pathology and Audiology at Teachers College, Columbia University in the area of geriatric communicology. I will close with a few words on the evolving interest of society in the goals of care for the elderly.

THE FIELD

The field of speech and language pathology and audiology is distinctively concerned with the study of speech-language-hearing processes, their disorders, and their management. The professional organization that represents the field is known as the American Speech-Language-Hearing Association (ASHA) and was incorporated in 1925.

The association publishes two major journals, the *Journal of Speech and Hearing Disorders* begun in 1936 and the *Journal of Speech and Hearing Research* in 1958, and an abstracts journal entitled *DSH Abstracts* begun in 1960.

The field also has a Council on Professional Standards and a Board of Examiners in Speech Pathology and Audiology (BESPA). Under BESPA are included the Clinical Certification Board (CCB),

Edward D. Mysak, PhD, is Professor and Chairman, Department of Speech and Language Pathology and Audiology, Teachers College, Columbia University.

the Professional Services Board (PSB), the Education and Training Board (ETB), and the Continuing Education Board (CEB). Respectively, these boards are responsible for monitoring the professional standards of individuals, clinics, master's degree programs, and programs offering continuing education.

There are approximately 40,000 members in ASHA, and it is estimated that this number will double in the next ten years or so. Practitioners in the field are expected to hold the Certificate of Clinical Competence in either speech-language pathology (CCC-SP) or audiology (CCC-A) as well as state licenses in their respective areas. Almost all states now have licensure laws in speech pathology and audiology. Speech-language pathologists and audiologists may be found teaching or performing research in universities and colleges, or practicing in school systems, rehabilitation centers, and hospitals. An increasing number may also be found in private practice.

The formal concern of ASHA in the effects of aging on speech-language-hearing processes may be traced to the establishment of the Committee on Communication Problems of the Aging in the early 1960's. It may be interesting to note that in the early sixties, bibliographies concerning communication problems of the aging included no more than 15 or so entries specifically concerned with speech or hearing, with the majority devoted to hearing. My own interest dates back to 1957 when I began a study of vocal aging for my doctoral dissertation. Studies of aging processes and speech were almost non-existent at that time in the American literature in speech pathology.

THE DEPARTMENT

The Department of Speech and Language Pathology and Audiology at Teachers College, Columbia University has also had a long-standing interest in aging processes in speech and hearing. This interest and concern have been reflected in a number of ways.

One of the earliest activities in the department in the area of aging and communication was the establishment of a doctoral Fellowship in Speech Pathology at the Hebrew Hospital for the Chronic Sick in the Bronx, New York. Through this fellowship the speech and hearing service at the hospital was begun. A long line of excellent doctoral candidates have contributed to the development of this service. A large number of master's degree candidates doing their practicum with the elderly were also supervised by these doctoral fellows. Most importantly, the elderly at the hospital have been receiving, in addition to their general service and care, service and care for their precious gifts of speech and hearing. Later we began a formal training affiliation with the Beth Abraham Hospital in the Bronx.

Our Speech and Hearing Center has provided outreach programs in hearing care and management to nursing facilities and senior citizen centers in the areas that are without such services. The department also offers a course entitled Communication Problems among the Aging designed for non-specialists and one entitled Geriatric Communicology designed for specialists. An advanced, professional master's degree (the Ed.M.) is available in Geriatric Communicology, and a student may emphasize aging processes and speech and language or hearing.

Research done in the department includes work on hearing impairment and social isolation, voice onset time and aging, perception of oral-verbal communication by residents of institutions for the chronically ill, and the development of a hearing handicap scale for the elderly.

SOCIETY

Relative to society's concern with the elderly, I would like to believe that there has been a slow but steady evolution in goals of care from emphasis on the more bodily needs to that of psychosocial and communicative needs.

Someone once described levels of care in terms of time binding, energy binding, space binding, self-binding, and society binding. The goals of time binding are to keep the individual alive, to slow any progressive diseases, and to prevent secondary problems. The primary caregivers at this level are the physicians and nurses using surgery, drugs, and various appliances. The goals of energy binding are concerned with the vegetative functions of breathing, swallowing, and eliminating. The primary caregivers are again the physician and nurse, with the speech pathologist taking on an ever increasing responsibility in the areas of breathing and swallowing. The goals of space binding are head control, trunk control (sitting), arm control (reach and grasp), and for these functions there are the physical therapists, occupational therapists, speech clinicians (re head and trunk control), and nurses. The goals of self-binding relate to small muscle control involved in eating, toileting, dressing, and communicating. The primary caregivers here are the occupational therapists, nurses, speech pathologists, and audiologists. Finally, the goals of society binding are to help make the individual intellectually and emotionally content with the degree of occupational and recreational proficiency which he or she can attain. The primary caregivers here are the psychologist, social worker, speech pathologist, and audiologist.

It is gratifying indeed to note that more and more residences for the elderly are beginning to invest more of their resources into furthering goals of care on the self-binding and society binding levels. To more and more specialists and to more and more families of residents the essence of successful aging is to maintain good intracommunication and good intercommunication among the elderly.

On that note, I look forward, as I know all of you are, to listening to and learning from the distinguished participants in this most important conference on Aging and Communication.

Hearing and Hearing Impairment in the Elderly

Ira M. Ventry

In the next few minutes I am going to discuss hearing impairment and aging. The first topic deals with the prevalence of hearing impairment in the aged, and let me assure you that hearing impairment among the aged is probably one of the most common problems, if not the most common, that older people face. There are a variety of prevalence estimates that describe hearing loss in the aged, and let me mention some of them. For all ages, the prevalence of significant hearing impairment is about 7%. For ages 65–74, the prevalence of hearing impairment increases from 7% to about 23%, and for people 75 years of age and over, the prevalence of hearing impairment is on the order of 40%. I should note that these prevalence estimates vary somewhat from study to study, but this gives you some idea of the changes in hearing sensitivity that take place as a function of age. It is also important to note that the elderly suffer significant hearing loss in both the low frequencies and the high frequencies, with loss in the highs being greater than that in the low frequencies. The implications of this high frequency hearing loss will be presented later.

Change in hearing sensitivity as a function of aging has been well documented in a number of studies, even though the exact prevalence or incidence figures vary from study to study. We also have some data with respect to the prevalence of hearing impairment in special populations. A recent study of low income elderly demonstrated that 75% had some degree of hearing impairment, with 28% of the sample having moderate to profound difficulty. Another special population that has received some attention in the

Ira M. Ventry, PhD, was Professor, Department of Speech and Language Pathology and Audiology, Teachers College, Columbia University.

literature is that of nursing home residents. Unfortunately, the data for nursing home residents are extremely varied, and the estimates of hearing impairment among nursing home residents range from about 9% in one study to over 90% in other studies. Several reasonably controlled studies, however, suggest that a fairly conservative prevalence figure based on audiometric testing of nursing home residents is on the order of 50%; thus, one out of every two nursing home residents is likely to have a significant hearing impairment.

Let me give you some summary statements about hearing impairment in the elderly. These are generalizations, but they hold true for most elderly people. First, hearing sensitivity, as we have seen, decreases with increasing age. Secondly, in the typical aged ear, there is no major difference between ears; that is, the elderly person generally has the same hearing impairment in both ears. Another important finding is that the sensitivity loss is greater in the high frequencies than in the low frequencies. Severity of loss is somewhat greater in males than in females, and there is evidence that suggests that there is a decrease in the ability to understand speech with increasing age, especially under difficult listening conditions.

What are the implications of these findings? First, hearing impairment can affect communication behavior. Second, hearing impairment can serve to create other problems. We are very interested, and have been for some time, in trying to determine how many people are misidentified as being demented when, in fact, they have serious hearing impairment rather than senile dementia. Hearing impairment can serve as an obstacle to successful medical treatment. Hearing loss in the aged can affect psycho-social behavior. The two most common consequences of hearing impairment in the aged are depression and withdrawal. Hearing loss in the aged can strain family relations. We have all had experience with individuals in our family who have had significant hearing impairment which has created all kinds of difficulty for the family. Hearing impairment can also severely limit or restrict previously enjoyed activity. The individual no longer goes to church or attends parties, and so on. Making it an even more difficult problem is the fact that the hearing impairment in aging is insidious in onset and is invisible to the naked eye. It frequently goes undetected because the symptoms may mimic other problems. Hearing impairment, then, is a problem afflicting the elderly, a problem that can have important consequences for the individual and his/her family.

Let me just quickly go over the parts of the auditory system that are involved in presbycusis; presbycusis is the term that is used to label hearing impairment that results from aging.

Outer ears are what you see on a person's head. The aged frequently have problems with their outer ears. The most important problem is impacted cerumen. It is interesting how a number of hearing problems can be "cured" when impacted cerumen is removed. Even though the patient's cerumen may be removed, he may still have a significant hearing impairment that is unrelated to the impacted wax.

The next part of the system that concerns us is the middle ear; the outer ear and the middle ear are involved in conducting the sound from the outside to the brain. Here, the research suggests that there are no major changes in the middle ear mechanisms of the elderly person. This does not mean, however, that the elderly person cannot have ear problems such as otitis media, or otosclerosis, or infections. But, generally speaking, the middle ear mechanism appears to be unaffected by the aging process.

The major problem with the elderly lies in the inner ear and beyond. The inner ear translates the mechanical input provided by the middle ear to electrical impulses in a very complicated way. Essentially the sequence is from the cochlea which is a receptor mechanism to the eighth nerve to the lower brain stem and on up through the higher auditory pathways. Most of the hearing impairment in presbycusis is sensorineural; that is, it involves the cochlea and the more central auditory mechanisms.

The basic problem in presbycusis is that there is a reduction in sensory cells as well as in neural tissue and these reductions affect the transmission, reception, and perception of sounds. It must be remembered, however, that the loss of hearing due to aging may also be aggravated by non-aging factors. Such factors include long-term exposure to noise, ototoxic drugs, ear disease, and the like. In fact, presbycusis is probably best understood as the cumulative effect of a number of disorders or insults, all contributing to the degeneration of the auditory mechanism.

Generally speaking, there is no medical treatment available these days to cure presbycusis. There are, however, a number of non-medical treatments and management procedures that will be discussed later that can be of great help to the elderly person with a hearing problem.

Let me briefly describe how we go about identifying a person with a hearing problem, and some of the measurements we take of a person with a hearing loss. The first step, obviously, in the whole rehabilitation process is to identify the person with the hearing problem. Ideally, the identification process should take place by means of formal hearing tests. Frequently that is not possible. In lieu of formal testing, there are some behavioral signs that people should look for that would suggest that the individual does indeed have a hearing problem. Here are some of these behavioral indications: frequently requests repetitions; misunderstands or is confused about what is said; reports that "I can't hear" or that "things need to be louder for me"; reports difficulty via family members or a person familiar with the individual (a nurse, social worker); turns up the television or radio; and avoids previously enjoyed social situations. These are some of the behavioral cues that suggest the possibility of a hearing problem.

In a recent study of the elderly, a 6-item questionnaire was developed that seems to be rather well correlated to sensitivity loss. The 6 items may be useful in identifying individuals with a hearing problem. They are: (1) "Have you ever owned a hearing aid?" If the person answers "yes" to that question, he/she is likely to have a significant hearing problem. (2) "Do you find that people tend to speak too softly?" Again, a "yes" answer would suggest that the person may have a hearing problem. (3) "Can you carry on a conversation with one other person when you are in a noisy place, such as a restaurant or at a party?" (4) "Are you 75 years of age or older?" (5) "Do you feel that any difficulty with your hearing inhibits or hampers your personal or social life?" (6) "Do people tell you that you speak too softly?" If there are "yes" responses to 3 or more of the questions, the chances are rather great that the individual has a significant hearing impairment and requires follow-up attention.

The most precise way to identify people with a hearing impairment is to initiate a hearing screening program; that is, a formal hearing testing program. Such a program is designed to identify quickly individuals who need follow-up services by providing fail-pass information on large numbers of people. Several major considerations, however, should be kept in mind in developing or initiating a hearing screening program. First of all, the hearing screening tests should be given by people who have been trained in administering the tests. I assure you that the older person is not that easy to test, either in screening or in a more elaborate testing situation. Another consideration is that in screening the elderly, screening levels (that is, the pass/fail levels) have to be adjusted upward. In other words, the fail criterion becomes more lenient to account for the fact that many elderly people have hearing impairment. If we use the same pass/fail criterion as we do for young adults, we will fail a large number of people who, in fact, may not be handicapped by their hearing loss. The test environment should be relatively quiet. Ideally, people tested should have their ears examined prior to the test to make certain that there is no impacted cerumen. Finally, and this is most important, any screening programs must have a well-defined referral system that can deal with individuals who fail the screening program. It makes no sense to identify an individual with a problem and then do nothing about it. Probably the most important part of this whole identification process is to make certain that there is a referral system that leads to the management of the individual with the hearing impairment.

A hearing screening program should also be complemented by some type of hearing handicap assessment; what is meant by this is that not all people with hearing impairment are handicapped by the impairment. There are vast differences among people in the way they react to or are affected by their hearing loss; two individuals with the same degree of hearing loss may have significantly different handicaps. In addition, there are people who pass a hearing screening but feel handicapped by their sensitivity loss, as well as people who fail a hearing screening but experience little or no handicap. Thus, the most meaningful and effective identification program should include a pure-tone screening test as well as an assessment of self-perceived handicap.

If an individual fails the screen, it is essential that he/she receive a follow-up audiological evaluation. The purpose of the evaluation is to determine the type of hearing impairment that exists and to quantify the extent and degree of hearing loss. Another important purpose of the audiologic evaluation is to determine the need for aural rehabilitation, including the determination of the need for a hearing aid, for counseling, for hearing therapy, and so forth.

Let me conclude. First, hearing impairment is a common consequence of aging. It is not reversible, but it can be managed. Second, hearing impairment, if unrecognized, can have dramatic effects on the elderly person. These effects include isolation, depression, and family strife. Third, hearing screening programs can be implemented in a variety of settings. Screening programs should be established to identify individuals with significant hearing impairment or handicap who should receive a complete audiologic evaluation. Fifth, the audiologic evaluation not only identifies the nature and degree of impairment but helps determine the client's candidacy for aural rehabilitation. Let me conclude with this excerpt from a report in one of our journals. The audiologist's client is describing what it is like to be old and hearing impaired:

> It is frightening to be 72 years old and gradually losing your hearing. You begin to wonder what is going to become of you. You feel frightened and alone when you hear people talking and can't understand the things they are saying. When I found out it was my hearing I felt a little better about myself, but that didn't solve the problem. I do want to hear what my grandchildren are saying. More than anything I want to enjoy myself again when I go to church or get together with my family or just when friends come over for coffee. I don't feel much use to anyone anymore and talking is most of all that I have left. When you can't participate in talks with family and friends there isn't much else to do but go away from it all.[1]

Thank you.

---

[1]From *Conversation: The Aging Speak*, Hull, R., *ASHA*, Vol. 22, 6, 1980.

Rehabilitation
of the Hearing Impaired Elderly

Barbara E. Weinstein

The sensorineural hearing loss associated with the aging process (i.e., presbycusis) is generally not amenable to medical intervention. Accordingly, alternative methods have evolved to minimize the communicative distress experienced by the hearing impaired elderly (Maurer & Rupp, 1979). Contrary to popular belief, the provision of a hearing aid and participation in a comprehensive aural rehabilitation program can assist the older adult to cope with and compensate for the hearing loss.

Individuals with a hearing impairment and a self-perceived hearing handicap will gravitate toward a rehabilitation program following the initial audiological evaluation. Typically, upon the completion of audiometric testing, the audiologist will recommend a hearing aid evaluation if the likelihood of medical resolution of the hearing problem is minimal. At the hearing aid evaluation a patient's performance with several hearing aids is compared using speech and tonal stimuli. At the completion of the comparative hearing aid trials, the audiologist and client will decide on the most appropriate amplification device. I should note that prior to the hearing aid evaluation, the client should be examined by an ear specialist to secure a medical diagnosis or to rule out medical contraindication to amplification. I should note that while consultation with a physician is mandated by the Food and Drug Administration (FDA), an audiological evaluation is not. However, medical and audiological interaction before the patient makes contact with the commercial product could safeguard the consumer (Freeman & Sinclair, 1981).

Following provision of amplification, the elderly individual

Barbara E. Weinstein, PhD, is Assistant Professor, Teachers College, Department of Speech-Language Pathology and Audiology, Columbia University.

should enroll in an aural rehabilitation program. The three components of a comprehensive rehabilitation program should include:

a. the *hearing aid orientation* wherein one is familiarized with the components, general operation, and maintenance of the hearing aid,
b. *speechreading and auditory* training sessions designed to train the new hearing aid user to maximize communication abilities in difficult listening situations, and
c. *educational and informational* counseling sessions to assist the individual to cope with problems related to the hearing loss (Garstecki, 1981).

The aural rehabilitation program is usually instituted on an individual or a group basis depending upon the needs of the client. Each has its advantages and disadvantages; while group therapy offers an excellent support system, it may fail to provide the intensive training one may find in individual therapy (Kaplan, 1979).

Several factors will influence the benefits to be derived from amplification and aural rehabilitation. First, the rehabilitation program must be comprehensive in scope. For example, if a hearing aid is dispensed in the absence of adequate follow-up (e.g., hearing aid orientation), prognosis for success will be guarded. Another factor that will influence ultimate adjustment to a hearing aid is the attitude of the potential hearing aid user (Maurer & Rupp, 1979). He/she must be motivated toward improving the existing condition. If not, the hearing aid will be consigned a space in the dresser drawer or the garbage! It is incumbent on health care professionals working with the elderly to take advantage of every opportunity to promote a positive attitude toward self-management of the hearing problem (Garstecki, 1981). Another prognostic factor is the age of the patient when purchasing the hearing aid. To explain, general adaptability tends to decrease with age. Accordingly, as the potential hearing aid user approaches 75 years and above, the prognosis for adjustment will decrease (Maurer & Rupp, 1979). Of course, there are exceptions to this rule. Unfortunately, individuals often postpone the decision to purchase a hearing aid and consequently have difficulty making the demanding adjustment to amplification.

Hearing impaired elderly individuals should be encouraged to explore the possibility of procuring a hearing aid while they are still able to adapt and willing to make the necessary effort (Berkowitz, 1975). Similarly, many individuals wait until the hearing loss becomes so severe that they become withdrawn, isolated, inattentive, and, in many cases, out of contact with the environment (Maurer & Rupp, 1979). Since some of the behavioral manifestations of severe hearing loss overlap with those observed in organic mental syndrome, such individuals may be inadvertently labeled "senile." It should be noted that the behavioral correlates of severe hearing loss are often instrumental in the decision to institutionalize. I might add that I have worked with several institutionalized patients whose medical diagnosis of "organic mental syndrome" was reversed following the provision of amplification. In addition, there have been numerous reports in the audiological literature of such cases (Ronholt, 1968).

Two questions audiologists are constantly called on to respond to are "what accounts for the reluctance on the part of the elderly to purchase a hearing aid?" and "why the skepticism about the benefits to be derived from amplification?" Cost is probably one factor, misconceptions another, and social stigma a third. Many older adults have been told by their family physician that persons with "nerve deafness" cannot wear a hearing aid. This simply is not the case, thanks to the technological advances in the hearing aid industry. In fact, success with a hearing aid is, in many cases, less dependent on the severity of the type of hearing loss and more a function of the desire to wear a hearing aid (Freeman & Sinclair, 1981). Hearing aids are not yet as fashionable as eyeglasses even though the lifestyle benefits can be as dramatic as those derived from eyeglasses (Maurer & Rupp, 1979). Hearing aids cannot function the way glasses do. Eyeglasses restore vision to normal; hearing aids simply do not. Performance with a hearing aid is constrained by the' frequency selective nature of the sensorineural hearing loss. Hearing loss is not a visible handicap, but to Helen Keller and others the emotional impact of a hearing loss can be greater than the loss of sight (Maurer & Rupp, 1979). "Loss of vision separates people from things, the tragedy of hearing loss is that it separates people from each other" (Maurer & Rupp, 1979, p. 101).

What is a hearing aid? A hearing aid is merely a miniature public address system. It is a device which increases the loudness of a signal and delivers it to an impaired ear. Sensorineural hearing loss results in a loss of hearing for frequencies important to the perception of speech and loss of the ability to distinguish one sound from another. Hence, the patient suffers from a loss of clarity in addition to a loss of loudness. The hearing aid will make the signal louder; however, it cannot rectify the difficulty the sensorineural impaired ear has in discriminating among different speech sounds. A hearing aid is not selective, it amplifies speech and non-speech sounds, including environmental noise. The new hearing aid user must be trained to separate the speech from the noise, and, given the limitations inherent in hearing aids, realistic expectations must be set.

Several different types of hearing aid arrangements are available to the consumer. Each system has its advantages and disadvantages. The choice of the most appropriate hearing aid is a function of electroacoustic variables, listening needs, type and severity of the hearing loss, speech discrimination ability, physical capabilities, and a host of other factors.

The internal components of most hearing aids are the same, the location of the parts distinguishes one hearing aid from the next. Thus, a body aid which is worn on the body, a behind-the-ear aid which is worn behind the ear, an in-the-ear aid which sits directly in the ear, and an eyeglass hearing aid, which is part of the temple portion of the eyeglasses, consist of a microphone, amplifier, receiver, battery, and an earmold. The microphone picks up the sound wave and converts it to an electrical signal, the amplifier takes power from the battery to amplify the signal and in turn the earphone/receiver changes the signal back into acoustic energy so that the sound can travel through the tubing to the earmold and into the ear. The total package ranges in price from $180 to $500, depending on the type of hearing aid and the person from whom the hearing aid is purchased.

The battery is the power source and is critical to the operation of the hearing aid. The battery should be changed on a regular basis (e.g., every 5–7 days), as a dead battery often accounts for an apparently malfunctioning hearing aid. Inserting new batteries on a regular basis is especially important in long-term care facilities where the patient may be unable to change the battery or to notify a staff member when in need of a new battery.

The earmold, or the plastic insert which conducts the amplified sound from the hearing aid into the ear canal, is another important component of the hearing aid. The selection of the earmold is of great import in the hearing aid evaluation, as rejection of a hearing aid is often linked to a poorly fitting earmold (Freeman & Sinclair, 1981). The annoying high pitched squeal, otherwise known as acoustic feedback, which is often heard when standing next to a hearing aid user, is most probably attributable to a poorly fitting earmold. If the earmold is not resting securely in an individual's ear, a slight push on the earmold will secure it and eliminate the annoying feedback. Placing the earmold in the ear and positioning the hearing aid can be a most frustrating task for the new hearing aid recipient. Proper instruction on earmold insertion will maximize the probability of a successful hearing aid fitting. Many elderly individuals will be able to position the hearing aid securely, and so it is important that a significant other participate in the aural rehabilitation process from the outset. The presence of a support person during the orientation and counseling sessions will facilitate the transfer of information and will, thus, be critical to the success of the intervention program. In the case of the institutionalized patient, the burden will fall on the staff member. In-service training programs must be conducted on a regular basis if therapeutic endeavors are to be meaningful (Lubinski, 1981). Staff members should be trained to: troubleshoot hearing aids to detect problems, to position the hearing aid securely in the patient's ear, and to communicate effectively with the patients. I should note that in-service training sessions should be offered on a regular basis to nurses, occupational, physical, recreational therapists, and any other allied health professionals working with the elderly.

The goal of the hearing aid orientation sessions is to establish realistic expectations from amplification. The client should be made aware of the advantages and disadvantages inherent in hearing aid use. For example, the hearing aid may not be beneficial during difficult listening situations, such as group conversations and in the presence of environmental noise. The new hearing aid user must be trained to identify the situations wherein he/she can experience success and should be encouraged to function in easy listening situations (Garstecki, 1981).

Speechreading and auditory training sessions are critical components of the aural rehabilitation process as well. The focus of these sessions is to encourage the patient to use all sensory modalities to assist in message perception. Similarly, significant others should be trained to assist in facilitating the communication process. Since facial expression, body gestures, and lip movements assist in assigning meaning to the vocal output, the following set of rules should be applied when speaking to the hearing impaired (Maurer & Rupp, 1979; Garstecki, 1981):

- face the listener,
- keep mouth unobstructed and refrain from eating or drinking while conversing,
- do not overarticulate as this may distort the sounds of speech,
- do not speak directly into the ear as this denies the listener the visual cues necessary to supplement audition.

In addition:

- maintain a close distance (i.e., 6–9 feet),
- speak at a slightly greater than normal intensity,
- speak at a normal rate but not too fast.

Finally, it is incumbent on both the listener and speaker to create an ideal environment for communication to take place. For example, distracting noises (e.g., television, stereo) should be avoided by moving to a less confusing area. By practicing these "small courtesies," one can assist the older adult to maximize communication abilities in difficult listening situations. An unexpected bonus—the need for repetition in the communication exchange will be significantly reduced (Garstecki, 1981).

Unfortunately, some elderly individuals may not be candidates for amplification due to physical problems, financial constraints, hearing loss severity, or lack of motivation. A few commercial products are available for individuals who fall into one of these categories. Ear trumpets, including speaking tubes or collapsible horns, are reportedly of some value to the hearing impaired. These non-electric units concentrate energy from the speaker's voice at the level of the listener's ear. Many users who are unable to use or afford conventional hearing aids report high satisfaction with these units (Maurer & Rupp, 1979).

A device known as a SPACE aid (Situational/Personal Acoustic Communication Equipment) has been gaining some popularity (Vaughn & Gibbs, 1982). Although the SPACE aid lacks the fidelity, frequency range, and gain of conventional hearing aids, they are preferable to a defective auditory system. A SPACE aid consists of a microphone, amplifier, headphone, and a power supply. This device amplifies the speech signal, thereby facilitating communication. The components are available from Radio Shack at a reasonable cost of approximately $60. Nursing home residents with a propensity toward losing hearing aids are ideal candidates for the SPACE aid. Similarly, if a hearing aid is contraindicated due to one's mental status or lack of independent function, the SPACE aid should be considered. Finally, health professionals, including nurses, social workers, and staff physicians, report that the SPACE aid facilitates the flow of interviews which are often strained in the absence of an amplification device.

One additional device worth describing is the telephone amplifier. Bell Telephone manufactures volume control headsets which allow the listener to adjust the intensity level of the speech signal coming through the earpiece. The headset, a thumb-operated wheel located in the center of the telephone headset, is available from Bell Telephone on a monthly rental basis (Maurer & Rupp, 1979). In addition, portable volume control amplifiers, which can be placed directly over the earpiece of the telephone receiver, can be purchased for a nominal amount from various hearing aid supply companies and Radio Shack. These portable devices allow the hearing impaired individual to adjust the intensity of the speech signal to an optimal listening level.

CONCLUSION

In closing, I would like to emphasize that provision of amplification and aural rehabilitation is one step toward assisting the elderly to achieve the satisfaction formerly attained through interpersonal contact. In short, the provision of a hearing aid can add life to the years of the hearing impaired elderly.

REFERENCES

Berkowitz, A. Audiologic rehabilitation of the geriatric patient. *Hearing Aid Journal,* 1975, *8,* 30–34.

Freeman, B., & Sinclair, J. Hearing aids for the elderly. In D. Beasley & G. Albyn Davis (Eds.), *Aging: Communication processes and disorders.* New York: Grune and Stratton, 1981.

Garstecki, D. ´Aural rehabilitation for the aging adult. In D. Beasley & G. Albyn Davis (Eds.), *Aging: Communication processes and disorders.* New York: Grune and Stratton, 1981.

Kaplan, H. Development, composition and problems with elderly aural rehabilitation groups. In M. Henoch (Ed.), *Aural rehabilitation in the elderly.* New York: Grune and Stratton, 1979.

Lubinski, R. Programs in home health care agencies and nursing homes. In D. Beasley & G. Albyn Davis (Eds.), *Aging: Communication processes and disorders.* New York: Grune and Stratton, 1981.

Maurer, J., & Rupp, R. *Hearing and aging.* New York: Grune and Stratton, 1979.

Ronholt, R. The work of an audio-educator in a large geriatric department in Copenhagen. In G. Liden (Ed.), *Geriatric audiology.* Stockholm: Almquist and Wiksell, 1968.

Vaughn, G., & Gibbs, S. Alternative and companion listening devices for the hearing impaired. In R. Hull (Ed.), *Rehabilitative audiology.* New York: Grune & Stratton, 1982.

Normal and Disordered Speech and Voice

Carol N. Wilder

INTRODUCTION

In the preceding two chapters, human communication was considered in terms of hearing, e.g., the reception or input of an intended message. But for communication to become a two-way process, several other steps are required. Through a complexity of mental processes, meaning must be extracted from the acoustic input, and a meaningful, relevant output message formulated. These processes are often subsumed under the heading of "language" functions. The output message must then be translated into the physiologic processes of vocalization and articulation which result in those acoustic signals known as "speech." For purposes of discussion, speech and language processes will be treated separately in the next two chapters. However, it should be understood that this separation is somewhat arbitrary because in many respects, speech and language are inextricably linked.

Speaking is such an integral part of our existence that we rarely stop to consider how much of our social, psychological, and even societal well-being is dependent on it. Even less often do we stop to consider how infinitely complex are the neuromotor processes on which speech is based. It is less surprising that speech disorders may occur than it is that speech develops normally and remains at least functionally adequate throughout the life span for most people. However, when speech is impaired, or when intelligible speech requires a disproportionate amount of effort, the impact on quality of life is profound.

The purposes of this chapter are: (1) to provide an overview of

Carol N. Wilder, PhD, is Clinical Associate, Adjunct Associate Professor, Teachers College, Columbia University.

factors which may affect normal speech production, (2) to describe the potential effects of biologic aging on the various components of the speech system, (3) to identify specific speech disorders prevalent in this population, and (4) to consider the impact of reduced speech efficiency on the communication of the elderly.

FACTORS WHICH INFLUENCE SPEECH PRODUCTION

Speech is often described as being produced by three systems: (1) the respiratory system which provides the basic power source for speech, (2) the phonatory system, in which the larynx provides the sound source for voice, and (3) the articulatory/resonatory system which modulates the voiced or voiceless airstream into the acoustic waveforms perceived as speech.

However, we have recently come to appreciate the fact that these components of speech production cannot be thought of as separate functional entities. Instead, they should be considered subsystems of a speech output mechanism which functions as a single coordinated and interactive unit for even the simplest utterances. Thus speech is perhaps best viewed as a complex motor act, probably the most complex motor act in which most people ever engage. It requires precise coordination of many different muscle groups in terms of range, velocity, direction, and timing of movements. Happily, we are usually unconscious of this fact while we are talking, and the speech flows automatically while we concentrate on the content or meaning of the message we wish to transmit. We take this amazing motor skill completely for granted—until something upsets it.

The extent and complexity of the speech system make it suscepti-ble to the influence of a variety of factors. The system involves much of the body, extending from the pelvic girdle upward through the craniofacial complex. Efficient speaking patterns (which may be roughly defined as the most intelligible output per unit of effort) are dependent not only on the structural integrity of the many system components, but also on the integrity of central and peripheral neural control mechanisms. (Many of us have had firsthand ex-perience with a reduction in speech efficiency caused by impaired neural control mechanism; recall the conscious effort to speak intelligibly when under the influence of oral anesthesia.) Speech production is also influenced by the autonomic nervous system, as can be attested to by anyone who has experienced "stage fright," wherein the mouth goes dry and it is difficult to control breathing. Because of its influence on metabolic factors, speech can be influenced by changes in or malfunction of the endocrine system. Indeed, the effects of endocrine malfunction on the larynx can be quite dramatic.

The basic power source of speech, respiration, is affected by posture. Even gravity plays a role, because mechanically, the system functions differently in the upright posture than it does in the horizontal posture (a consideration which should be taken into account when evaluating or treating the speech of bedridden individuals). And to further complicate the picture, speech production may be significantly influenced by affective states and general physical condition. The listener, consciously or unconsciously, gains clues as to the speaker's mood or health status. Indeed, such judgments are often made on the basis of two or three words of greeting when the listener knows the speaker well. Thus we should view speech not only as a complex motor act, but also as a sensitive indicator of the speaker's general physical and emotional status. This is an important consideration for all health professionals who interact with the aging.

BIOLOGIC AGING AND THE SPEECH SYSTEM

Speech is also a rather sensitive indicator of age itself. Studies have shown that untrained listeners can make remarkably accurate estimates of the chronological ages of healthy adult speakers, just on the basis of recorded speech samples (Shipp & Hollien, 1969; Ryan & Burk, 1974). Although we are only beginning to achieve an understanding of the acoustic cues which contribute to perceptual judgments of agedness (Kent & Burkard, 1981), it can safely be said that in general, people tend not only to "look" but to "sound" their biologic ages. Some of the general features of biologic aging include: (1) reduced muscle bulk and strength, (2) increased fatiguability of muscles, (3) changes in mucosal tissue, (4) increased fragility of blood vessels, (5) decreased structural elasticity, (6) arthritis, (7) osteoporosis, and (8) decrements in sensory function. Each of these biologic changes may affect the speech system. Further, even if only one of its components is adversely affected, the speech system is so highly interactive that the function of its other components will be influenced.

For continuous speech, air must be moved into the lungs easily and rapidly, otherwise the flow of communication will be slowed. Further, egression of air from the lungs must be precisely controlled so that air pressure remains within a rather narrow range of tolerance. If it does not, speech will be of inappropriate loudness, and/or the length of the breath group may be altered. A number of the features of biological aging can make this respiratory task more difficult and effortful. For example, if osteoporosis and/or degeneration of the intervertebral discs give rise to senile kyphosis, the spinal curvature results in a change in the shape of the thorax, which reduces the mobility of the respiratory pump. Mobility may also be decreased by a stiffening of the joints by which the ribs are joined to the vertebral column and the sternum. The muscles which move the respiratory system may be weakened. The tissues of the system, in general, may become less elastic. This in itself reduces speech efficiency, because elastic recoil forces play an important role in speech respiration. In short, it may require more energy to move air and to control air pressure for speech at a time when there may be less energy available to the speaker.

Because the speech system components are interactive, having a less efficient power source immediately puts an extra load on the next system component, the larynx. This occurs at a time when vocal function may be affected by age-related changes in the larynx itself. The cartilages forming the framework for the larynx become ossified and more rigid. Mobility of the two pairs of laryngeal joints may be impaired by arthritic changes. The muscles which comprise the vocal cords lose bulk and become more easily fatigued. The mucosa lining the larynx becomes thinner and dryer, which not only alters the way in which the cords vibrate, but also makes them more susceptible to irritation and trauma. This greater irritability of tissue, together with the increasing incidence of respiratory problems in the elderly, often leads to excessive coughing and throat-clearing, which in themselves contribute to further laryngeal irritation. Because of increased fragility of blood vessels, there is often submucous hemorrhaging in response to such laryngeal abuse. It is not surprising that research suggests that vocal changes provide one of the major perceptual clues for identifying a speaker as aged (Ptacek & Sander, 1966; Ryan & Burk, 1974; Ryan & Capadano, 1978).

In the articulatory/resonatory component of the speech system, we find age-related biologic changes that may affect the entire oral environment. The oral mucosa becomes more susceptible to irritation, and production of saliva is altered. Loss of dentition may directly affect articulation, and ill-fitting dentures are common. Structural changes altering the relationship of the upper and lower jaws may not only alter the lines of force of the articulatory muscles, but may alter the shape of the oral cavity sufficiently to change resonance characteristics. These several factors may combine to alter significantly the adaptation of the tongue to its oral environment.

Neurologic changes are also a common feature of biologic aging. Although there is some disagreement in the literature about the effects of aging on central processes and neural transmission time, there is common agreement that sensory function is reduced. This is important because efficient neuromotor control of the speech system is not only contingent upon efferent signals to the muscles involved, but is also highly dependent on sensory feedback. While the importance of sensory feedback from the auditory system is obvious, feedback from receptors in the muscles, joints, and mucosa of the speech system is also essential to the smooth output of speech.

Although biologic aging may result in altered speech patterns, speech remains functionally adequate for most of the elderly. It may be less efficient in terms of intelligibility or effort level, but it serves in many communicative situations. This is due, in part, to the fact that the speech signal is highly redundant; there are many more acoustic cues available in the signal than the listener actually needs in order to decode the message. Moreover, even when the speech signal is considerably degraded (e.g., less intelligible), the listener is aided by knowledge of the topic (which makes certain words more probable), and by knowledge of the language (which makes certain sound sequences and word orders more probable than others). Another factor which allows for the maintenance of functional speech is that the biologic changes we have mentioned occur on different developmental schedules. They do not occur suddenly, simultaneously, or with equal severity of expression. More commonly, they occur in idiosyncratic combinations in different individuals, and their onset is so insidious that compensatory adjustments may be made unconsciously. However, another common feature of biologic aging is reduced plasticity of function, so that with advancing age, fewer compensatory adjustments may be available. In certain individuals, there may be a number of age-related changes in the speech system which individually are rather minor, but in the aggregate are beyond the person's capacity for spontaneous compensation. As a result, impaired intelligibility and/or heightened effort levels may make oral communication much more difficult, and speech may not always be adequate in certain communicative situations. Professional assistance may be needed to help the elderly speaker locate and use those compensatory adjustments that will maintain speech efficiency at the maximum possible level.

SPEECH DISORDERS PREVALENT IN THE ELDERLY

Neuropathologies, especially parkinsonism and cerebrovascular accidents, account for the largest number of speech pathologies in the elderly. For many years, such neuromotor speech disorders were grouped under the heading of dysarthria. However, so many different symptom complexes have been isolated that the heading has been pluralized, and the dysarthrias are defined as a group of related speech disorders resulting from disturbed motor control over the speech mechanism (Darley, Aronson, & Brown, 1975). In the dysarthrias, oral communication is impaired because of paralysis, weakness, abnormal tone, or incoordination of the muscles of the speech system. Occasionally, there are also what are called positive symptoms, that is, there are inappropriate or involuntary movements due to disinhibited activity of intact parts of the nervous system. Although a detailed categorization of symptom complexes is beyond the scope of this presentation, dysarthric symptoms may include inappropriate loudness, pitch, or rate of speech; impaired articulation; hypernasality; disturbed inflectional patterns; and an inability to sustain speech. To some listeners, dysarthric speech sounds bizarre, and is consciously or unconsciously associated with intoxication, mental retardation, or mental disorder. Because of this, dysarthria has sometimes contributed to erroneous diagnosis of dementia or other mental disorder. To avoid such errors, as well as to determine appropriate management procedures, it is very important to obtain a differential diagnosis from a qualified speech clinician whenever unusual speech patterns are observed.

There is another set of speech symptoms related to cerebrovascular disease which does not fall under the category of the dysarthrias. These speech symptoms are thought to be associated with damage to Broca's area in the speech-dominant hemisphere, and they include highly variable articulatory patterns, inaccurate sequencing of phonemes, disturbed prosodic patterns, and struggle behaviors associated with speech attempts. These symptoms seem to be related to an impairment in the central programming for positioning and sequencing muscle movements for the *volitional* production of phonemes. The operative term in this instance is "volitional"; there is no evidence of significant weakness, slowness, or incoordination in reflexive or automatic acts, and indeed automatic and reactive speech may be little impaired. Because of this feature, this set of speech symptoms is commonly called verbal apraxia, or apraxia of speech. This label has long caused controversy in the field of speech pathology. Those who are comfortable with the term "apraxia" consider the disorder to be simply a special type of motor speech disorder which is different from the dysarthrias. However, others believe that these symptoms reflect a motor programming component of language formulation, and therefore, they consider the term apraxia to be inappropriate. Still others take comfort from the fact that there is agreement on both sides of the controversy that the basis of the problem lies with motor programming.

Carcinoma, another disease prevalent in the elderly, may affect any part of the speech system, but the most commonly encountered speech pathology directly related to carcinoma is partial or total laryngectomy. Rehabilitative efforts for the elderly laryngectomee are sometimes too readily abandoned. Although there may be some very special management problems, an effective mode of communication can usually be developed with sufficient ingenuity and perseverance on the part of the clinician.

In the elderly, there is also increased incidence of respiratory disorders, such as obstructive lung disease, emphysema, and tuberculosis. When these conditions significantly alter respiratory behavior, they may result in problems with control of loudness, length of utterance, and intonation. Lesions involving the upper lobe of the left lung may impinge on the left recurrent laryngeal nerve, with consequent paresis or paralysis of the left vocal fold. The pathway of this nerve is such that it can also be affected by aneurysm of the aorta. Consequently, it is important for health professionals to be aware that at any age, *sudden* onset of a weak, breathy voice should be regarded as something of an emergency, and the larynx should be visualized by a physician as soon as possible. If vocal fold paralysis (particularly of the left fold) is observed, an etiological investigation should be undertaken immediately.

IMPACT OF REDUCED SPEECH EFFICIENCY

For speech to be considered maximally efficient, three things must occur: the message must be transmitted by the speaker with economy of effort, the message must reach the listener with all its communicative intent intact, and the message must be comprehended by the listener with minimal effort. A reduction in speech efficiency, whether due to a specific speech disorder or just to "normal" aging processes usually leads to less frequent use of the speech system. For example, if speaking requires an excessive amount of physical effort, the speaker may become fatigued; or if intelligibility is even slightly impaired and the intended message misunderstood, the speaker may become frustrated. In either case, the individual is negatively reinforced for attempts to speak, and hence may make fewer attempts to do so. From the listener's standpoint, trying to understand the inefficient speaker may be uncomfortably effortful or too time-consuming. In this case the listener, either consciously or unconsciously may elect to enter into fewer communicative contacts with that speaker. And consider the potential effects on communication of a situation frequently encountered among the elderly, that in which one partner of the communicative pair has a speech problem, while the other has a hearing problem! Whatever its cause, reduced speech efficiency usually leads to less frequent use of the speech system, and this, in a self-reinforcing cycle, can lead to even greater reduction in speech efficiency. Speech is a highly skilled motor activity. At any age, the less a skilled motor activity is performed, the greater the potential for loss of skill—as attested to by the old adage, "use it or lose it." One of the activities to which this adage is applicable is oral communication.

REFERENCES

Darley, F.L., Aronson, A.E. and Brown, J.R., *Motor Speech Disorders,* W.B. Saunders Co., Philadelphia, 1975.

Ptacek, P. and Sander, E., Age recognition from voice. *Journal of Speech and Hearing Research,* 1966, 9, 353-360.

Ryan, W. and Burk, K., Perceptual and acoustic correlates of aging in the speech of males. *Journal of Communication Disorders,* 1974, 7, 181-192.

Ryan, W. and Capadano, N., Age perceptions and evaluative reactions toward adult speakers. *Journal of Gerontology,* 1978, 33, 98-102.

Shipp, T. and Hollien, H., Perception of the aging male voice. *Journal of Speech and Hearing Research,* 1969, 13, 703-710.

Language Problems in the Elderly

A. Damien Martin

I am always a little hesitant to speak of language disorders in aging. This hesitation comes from a fear that I might contribute to two mistaken ideas about both language and aging: first, that language problems are always symptomatic of disease process; second, that aging itself is a disease rather than part of normal development.

I think it is important to specify immediately that "language disorders" may often be problems in communication arising from social and cultural factors rather than symptoms of neurological change. They may also, of course, be disruptions in communication from physiological change. In either case, the speech pathologist can be of service to the aging individual and to those who deal with him or her through, first, the identification of the problem and possible maintaining factors and, second, suggestions on how best to ameliorate these problems. I will avoid the use of the terms diagnosis and therapy as much as possible, even though they may be appropriate most of the time, because their use often contributes to an overriding medical view of communication problems faced by the aging.

Level of Reference

Any conscious attempt to change communication behavior must specify as clearly as possible the answer to three questions: What is the nature of normal functioning? What is the nature of the problem? and What is the nature of the ameliorative approach? While seemingly simple, straightforward, and obvious, the answers to these questions vary according to two major factors, the chosen level of reference and the theoretical model which underlies the examiner's

A. Damien Martin, EdD, is Director, Program in Speech Pathology and Audiology, New York University.

view. While the latter is important, any extensive examination of the role that different models may play in supplying different answers would take us too far afield in this discussion. However, an examination of level of reference may serve an heuristic purpose here.

Level of reference can be defined simply as the focus of discussion. In other words, it is what you are talking about. It is probably the one element in clinical and scholarly discussion that is most often unspecified, thus allowing for the proverbial mixing of apples and oranges.

For the speech pathologist, the two most important levels of reference are *information processing* and *communication.* In the former, the emphasis is on intrapersonal functioning; in the latter, interpersonal functioning. Entirely different definitions of normal functioning, the problem, and the corrective approach (or therapy) will depend on which is the focus of attention.

Since the schema proposed here should apply to all problems, and not just to ''language disorders,'' let us illustrate the application of the level of reference concept to individuals who are usually considered to have a speech rather than a language problem, laryngectomees.

In any discussion of the laryngectomized, normal functioning would probably be described with reference to anatomical and physiological integrity of the speech mechanism. The disorder or problem would then be defined with reference to the loss of speech skills as a result of an attack on that integrity through surgery. Therapy would usually be an attempt to replace the lost system with another ''voice'' producing mechanism, either esophageal speech or an artificial larynx.

Thus the answer to the first question might be that normal functioning is the efficient use of the vocal folds to modify the passage of air from the lungs to the pharyngeal, oral, and nasal resonating chambers to produce sound which can be modified in those same resonating chambers. The disorder might then be defined as the loss of the larynx with a concomitant loss of the normal sound producing mechanisms which underlie speech. Therapy would be the attempt to enable the individual to produce sound that could be used for speech.

(Two parenthetical observations: I am sure that speech and voice scientists can and will come up with better definitions. I also realize that information processing usually refers to cognition rather than what might be called the mechanical activity of speech. I am stretching the concept slightly for the purposes of illustrating by considering the production of speech sound to be the end result of an information processing activity.)

When we use communication as our level of reference, however, we have different results. Communication is an interaction between at least two participants. (For this discussion we will consider communication solely as human interaction. There are, of course, other interactions. For example, the design of a physical environment can and does provide messages to those who operate within that environment, affecting their performance on many levels.) If the focus is on interaction, we cannot attend solely to the individual. Therefore, it would be essential to examine and describe the effect that each participant has on the other. In the case of the laryngectomee, the focus would necessarily be on the listening skills of the other person, as well as on the speaking skills of the laryngectomee. This would affect any attempt to deal with problems of intelligibility in that a decision might be made to concentrate on improving the listening skills of the non-laryngectomized participant and to train the laryngectomized participant to attend to nonverbal cues which indicate non-comprehension on the part of the listener. Any one of a number of interaction models of communication, for example, those proposed by Muma (1975) or Watzlawick, Beavin, and Jackson (1967) could be used to formulate the necessarily different answers to one question.

LANGUAGE PROBLEMS

Much of the discussion that follows is based on earlier work in the area of aphasiology (Martin, 1979, 1980, 1981). This is not meant to imply that all elderly people are aphasic, nor that models of diagnosis and therapy in aphasia are always appropriate. However, some of the problems we see in the elderly do result from neurological change, and it is here that aphasiology can give us some guidelines on how to approach similar problems in the aged.

Information Processing

Language can be viewed in two ways, as a code and as a behavior. As a code, we can talk about nouns, verbs, adjectives, phrases, syntax, and so forth. As a behavior, we can describe what the individual does with that code.

The basic foundation for language behavior, whether expressive or receptive, is cognition. Cognition is all the process by which sensory information is transformed, reduced, elaborated, stored, recovered, and used (Neisser, 1966). Any use of the language code involves a number of different cognitive processes acting together.

With this as our starting point, normal functioning in language usage can be defined as the efficient action and interaction of the cognitive processes which support language behavior. The disorder that results from neurological change is then defined as the reduction of efficiency of the action and interaction of the cognitive processes which support language. Therapy is the attempt to excite and manipulate the action and interaction of the cognitive processes which support language behavior so as to maximize their effective usage (Martin, 1979). One important distinction between this definition of therapy and some others should be stressed. The goal is not seen as an attempt to return the individual to "normal" nor to "correct" or cure the problem. Rather, the goal is to help the individual to operate at the most efficient level of which he is capable.

Identification of the problem within these definitions would encompass the designation of one or more cognitive processes which are not operating with sufficient efficiency.

Let us take as a first example a cognitive process generally considered to be an important part of language behavior, short-term memory. One aspect of short-term memory is the ability to hold and process a message as it is being said. The amount of information we can hold while still processing efficiently is called auditory retention span. For example, if I say "Last night I had steak and french fries before I went to the movie and I had indigestion all during the show," one must process and retain the first part of the utterance while it is being said and hold on to it while receiving the rest of the sentence. Some individuals, either as a result of trauma, disease, or aging, find that they have a reduced capacity for processing language with reference to length. If a sentence is too long, such an individual may have difficulty and will lose part of the information.

In the case of the sentence given above, the individual in question might be able to process the first part of the sentence—"Last night I had steak and french fries"—but lose the latter two parts, a phenomenon that Wepman (1972) referred to as the "shutter effect." If the individual responds with "that's nice," the comment would seem inappropriate to the other participant while being absolutely appropriate to the received information. Similarly, the individual might process only the second part of the utterance—"I went to the movies last night"—and respond with "How was it?" The result of these apparently inappropriate remarks might be a mistaken view of the individual as confused, deaf, disoriented, etc.

Even more distressing and misleading may be the apparent "in and out" nature of the aging individual's responses. If the individual concerned were to process only the last of the utterance—"I had indigestion all during the show"—and answer "what a shame" or "did you take anything for it" or any number of apparently appropriate responses, the basic problem could be overlooked until the next occasion when the response does not seem to match expectations, with the resulting belief that the person goes "in and out." What seems to be inconsistent behavior is actually very consistent when one realizes the nature of the problem.

A number of other problems may arise from reduced efficiency in the processing of language information. Unfortunately, many of these problems are similar to those demonstrated by aphasics and the older person may be misdiagnosed. Even specialists sometimes forget that, as Freud pointed out years ago, such symptoms are common to everyone under certain conditions including stress, fatigue, intoxication, and so forth. Since the older person may be more prone to fatigue, stress of varying kinds, and is often taking medication for a variety of ills, the following symptoms may not be, indeed usually are not, symptoms of either aphasia or neurological damage. For this reason it is important that any diagnostic procedures be extensive, conducted over a period of time, and re-evaluated regularly.

A reduction in the efficiency of information processing capabilities may result in *word retrieval* problems. Thus, an individual may have difficulty remembering a name, a simple word, or even a short series of words. This difficulty can range from mild to severe. In the mild cases, the individual may comment that he or she does not remember names as well as before. Reaction to the difficulty can also be varied. Some accept lapses as consistent with other changes they have noticed. Others react with fear, frightened that the occasional difficulty may be a sign of advancing senility. In the latter case, overreaction can often exacerbate the problem as can be attested to by anyone who has desperately tried to remember somebody's name. We have all had the experience of not remembering a name and finally, after wracking our minds, giving up—and then remembering. If the older person is reacting negatively to difficulties in word retrieval, therapy should consist of reassurance as well as specific tasks directed toward improving retrieval skills.

Similar to word finding difficulty are *associative responses.* Here the individual produces an incorrect word, but one which is related to the desired word through a strong association. For example, one may say black for white, up for down, in for out, etc. Again, this is something that occurs in all individuals at sometime or other but may occur more often as the general system is reduced in efficiency. Since such errors often drastically change the meanings of the desired utterance, the individual may be judged as confused or rambling. Again, rather than direct work on more efficient word retrieval alone, the best strategy may be for the listener to model the utterance in such a way as to check meaning. To give a simple example, if the older person were to say, "I am going to see my daughter tonight," when it is a son who is visiting, one could say, "Your son, John, is coming to visit you tonight?" Such non-corrective responses serve three purposes: first, they enable the listener to decide whether or not the individual is indeed confused or has simply made an associative error; second, it provides a non-threatening model of the correct information; and third, the individual does not necessarily feel corrected.

The above are only samples of the kinds of errors that can occur in a system that has been generally reduced in efficiency. The speech pathologist, who conducts a thorough, ongoing diagnostic evaluation, can help those who work with the elderly to identify and deal with these and other problems. It is important to remember that lapses of memory, difficulty dealing with the information provided by others, and errors in speech and language are not necessarily signs of confusion or mental deterioration. They may only be the natural outcome of a number of factors related to the general reduction of efficiency in an aging system.

An information processing approach such as that described above has as its focus the problems of the elderly person. A second approach, where the emphasis is on communication, attends to the problems and difficulties of those who interact with the communicatively impaired older person.

Communication

It is important to remember that language is not synonymous with communication. Nor is it only a simple transfer of information coded linguistically. As Muma put it, communication

> . . . is more complicated than an active speaker talking to a passive listener. Both speaker and listener are active participants in formulating, perceiving, and revising messages until necessary adjustments are made in form, references, or psychological distance and acceptability in order to convey intended meaning(s). Both speaker and listener interact in a variety of feedback operations, including switching speaker-listener roles, to recode a message until consensus is reached not only about the essential meaning(s) but ways it could be most effectively and efficiently conveyed. (p. 299)

Communication is first and foremost a form of behavior.

> . . . one cannot *not* behave. Now if it is accepted that all behavior in an interactional situation has message value, i.e., is communication, it follows that no matter how one may try, one cannot not communicate. Activity or inactivity, words or silence, all have message value; they influence others and these others, in turn, cannot not respond to these communications and are thus themselves communicating. . . .Neither can we say that ''communication'' only takes place when it is in-

tentional, conscious or successful, that is when mutual understanding occurs. Whether message sent equals message received is an important but different order of analysis.
(Watzlawick, Beavin, & Jackson, 1967, 48-49)

A communication interaction, therefore, is a form of behavior in
which there is an exchange of messages.

The first stage of the speech pathologist's intervention in a communication context would thus be the education of all those who interact with the individual as to the nature of the problem. This first
step will hopefully lead to a diminution of mistaken messages in the
exchange.

Within the communication level of reference, our three essential
questions would be answered as follows: normal functioning is the
maintenance by *both* participants in a conversational exchange of
appropriate sender/receiver roles with maximum efficiency; the
problem is the disruption of that interaction through the failure of
either or *both* participants as a receiver or sender in the exchange.
Thus, if any elderly person had difficulties in communication
because of a reduction in auditory retention span, the problem is
viewed not just in the elderly individual, but with all those who interact with him or her.

The logical implication is that corrective action would be directed
toward *both* members of the interaction and not just the individual
who is perceived as being impaired. Therapy would then be defined
as the attempt to maximize and improve performance in both participants as both receivers and senders.

Let us continue with the example of reduced auditory retention
span to see how this might be implemented. If the individual has difficulty in managing messages beyond a certain length, one can help
him by changing the length of the messages. Thus, those who are
dealing with the individual could phrase the message so that the
elderly person with the difficulty can handle it. For example, "Last
night . . . I had steak and french fries . . . then we went to the
movies . . . And I had indigestion all during the show." The pauses
allow the individual with the reduced retention span to process the
message, and prepare for the next step.

An important aspect in this kind of intervention is the proper identification of the problem. It could be considered as condescending, and be counter-productive, to use this particular technique with an elderly individual who does not have a problem with reduced auditory retention span. It is essential that there be a close interaction between the speech pathologist and those significant others, including the professional gerontologist, who deal with the elderly.

CONCLUSION

One unfortunate side effect of what has been called the "medical model" has been the belief or attitude that problems must be dealt with solely by correcting what is perceived to be wrong with the individual. As we have seen above, often a problem may be alleviated by stressing the performance of another in the situation.

One of the major contributions the speech pathologist can make is in the identification of specific problems that are interfering with communication. There are batteries of tests, as well as the professional expertise of the speech pathologist, which can contribute to such identification. After the specific problem has been identified, the speech pathologist can then help in setting up the appropriate corrective or facilitatory action.

There is a great need, however, for interaction among all involved with the elderly individual. My experience at the Veterans Administration Hospital taught me that the observations of those who dealt most closely with the individual were essential to my work with that individual. We found that the greatest need was for the development of a common vocabulary and mechanisms for the sharing of information. This in turn led to an increased ability on our part to share our observations and hypotheses and to develop a common approach to the problems of the individual. The speech pathologist can bring his or her professional expertise to the identification of speech, language, and hearing problems in the elderly, can help in suggesting and developing corrective or facilitory procedures, and most importantly, can promote through interdisciplinary sharing the nature of communication problems in the aging.

REFERENCES

Martin, A.D. Levels of reference for aphasia therapy. In R. Brookshire (ed.), *Clinical aphasiology.* Minneapolis: BRK Publishers, 1979.

Martin, A.D. An examination of Wepman's thought centered therapy. In R. Chapey (ed.), *Language intervention strategies in adult aphasia.* Baltimore: Williams & Wilkins, 1980.

Martin, A.D. The role of theory in therapy: A rationale. *Topics in language disorders,* 4, 63-72, 1981.

Muma, J.R. The communication game: Dump and play. *J. Speech Hearing Dis.,* 40, 296-309, 1975.

Neisser, U. *Cognitive psychology.* New York: Appleton-Century-Crofts, 1966.

Watzlawick, P., Beavin, J., and Jackson, D. *Pragmatics of human communication.* New York: W. W. Norton, 1967.

Wepman, J. Aphasia therapy: A new look. *J. Speech Hearing Dis.,* 37, 203-214, 1972.

Management of Speech and Language Disorders in the Elderly: Some General Considerations

Carol N. Wilder

Although oral communication deficits are a significant feature of aging, there is often a curious reluctance to provide treatment. Some of the reasons for this reluctance may be associated with negative, often false assumptions related to the "agism" which is so pervasive in our society. One such assumption is that the elderly either don't *need* or don't *want* to communicate as much as they did when they were younger. Indeed, social isolation theorists suggest that withdrawal from communicative contacts is deliberate. Not everyone agrees with this theory, especially many of the elderly themselves. When their opinion is asked, they express great interest in having a variety of communication contacts, as well as regret over diminished opportunities or capacities for communication (Lubinski, 1979, 1981). Many of the elderly are surprised to learn that help may be available for their communication problems. Another widespread negative assumption holds that it is not worth the effort and expense to provide therapeutic services to old people, because you can't cure being old, and because they won't live that much longer anyway. Unsurprisingly, many of the elderly do not share this attitude, which totally begs the issue of quality of life for an unpredictable number of remaining years.

As individual practitioners and as a whole, the profession of speech-language pathology and audiology must shoulder some of the blame for any lack of remedial services for oral communication impairment in the elderly. One problem lies in the nature of the

Carol N. Wilder, PhD, is Clinical Associate, Adjunct Associate Professor, Teachers College, Columbia University.

etiology of the speech and language disorders in this population, which are usually related to neuropathology, structural change, or biologic aging. These underlying conditions tend to be irreversible, if not progressive. Some speech-language pathologists have been unwilling to undertake intensive therapy programs with elderly persons when the communication disorder was related to irreversible or progressive conditions because they felt it was not the best use of their professional time. On the other hand, some clinicians are highly motivated to work with patients with progressive diseases, but they are unable to do so because of policies of certain third party payment systems. However, even though restoration of oral communication to its premorbid condition may not be possible, communication *efficiency* can usually be improved. And in progressive conditions, therapeutic intervention often serves to maintain functionally adequate communication longer than would otherwise be possible, with consequent benefits for both patient and caregivers. Moreover, therapeutic attention to communication difficulties, in and of itself, appears to contribute substantially to the psychological well-being of many elderly persons.

Another source of reluctance to provide services for the elderly is that some speech-language pathologists feel inadequately prepared to deal with the complex issues presented by this population. Until recently, few training programs offered specific course work or practicum experience in geriatric communicology. Fortunately, a rapidly growing appreciation of the professional challenges posed by the elderly has resulted in a change in attitudes of both individuals and institutions within our field. At both national and state levels, standing committees on communication problems of the aging are charged with the development of standards for training and service delivery. More training programs are offering special course work and practicum experiences, and a few are offering specialization in geriatric communicology. Many continuing education experiences are available for the practicing clinician who wishes to acquire expertise with this population. Interest in providing diagnostic and remedial services for the elderly is also growing because the speech-language pathologist's role is expanding. It is no longer limited to narrowly defined communication disorders, but is equally concerned with maintaining the best possible communication function in the presence of biologic aging. Our involvement is no longer confined to the therapy room, but also extends to the entire communication environment, whether the elderly individual resides in the community or in an institution.

While the communication problems of the aged are of increasing concern to speech-language pathologists and audiologists, interest also seems to be growing in institutions and organizations serving the elderly. As institutions turn from a custodial to a therapeutic orientation, they are becoming cognizant of the fact that maximizing their residents' communication skills improves the quality of life for residents and staff alike. In many organizations, there is also a new emphasis on the provision of services which will either prevent institutionalization, or which will permit the return of institutionalized patients to the community. They are becoming aware that significant communication impairment may play a major role in determining whether someone becomes or remains institutionalized. For these reasons, management of communication problems is increasingly seen not as a luxurious afterthought, but as an essential component of comprehensive services for the elderly.

Specific details of diagnostic and remedial procedures are beyond the scope of this paper. However, there are several special features of which the reader should be aware. Typical management procedures must be especially adapted to take into account some of the physical, psychological, sociological, and environmental factors associated with aging. For example, it is very important that the diagnostic process be expanded beyond the typical one-on-one encounter in a relatively quiet, distraction-free room. This is because adequacy of oral communication is highly situation-dependent. The communication abilities of the elderly are even more susceptible than those of younger persons to situational factors such as ambient noise, time of day, positioning and posture of the speaker, positioning of the listener, and listener attitudes. If the evaluation is perceived as a "testing" situation, the resulting anxiety may adversely affect performance for some. For others, performance-affecting anxiety or distractibility may be engendered by any disruption in daily routine. Therefore, formal assessment must be augmented by environmental observation and close consultation with those who regularly interact with the subject.

Other psycho-social factors must also be considered in the selection of testing and therapy materials. In the current cohort of the elderly, in most metropolitan areas, for example, there is a relatively large number for whom English is a second (if not third or fourth) language, and there are also many who do not read at a high enough level to be comfortable with some widely used testing materials. However, in the search for simpler language, easier reading level, larger print, or simple illustrations, speech-language pathologists must be careful not to contribute to the infantilization which is so justly resented by many old people. In their search for such materials, speech-language pathologists have too often reverted to materials developed for young children without adequate consideration of their psychological impact on the older person.

Procedures must also be adapted to take features of biologic aging into account. For example, reduction in speed of response should be expected and allowed for, especially in test administration. To avoid fatigue, several shorter diagnostic sessions are preferable to the traditional single longer one, and it is best to schedule the most rigorous parts of the evaluation at those times of day when the subject is known to be at his/her best. This may require some flexibility on the part of caregivers. Dentures must be evaluated for their effect on speech. Age-related sensory deficits are also very important considerations. Testing and therapy materials must be adapted to accommodate any vision problems. And hearing status is perhaps the most important consideration of all. Since knowledge of hearing function is essential for accurate interpretation of speech-language performance, it is always advisable to obtain an audiologic evaluation prior to speech-language evaluation. If the subject has a hearing aid, the speech-language clinician must not only make sure that it is worn, but that it is actually working! In addition, conditions for lip-reading should be optimized by careful attention to lighting and positioning of subject and clinician. These communication-facilitating conditions are not only necessary for speech-language evaluation, but they should be thought of as essential to any type of assessment requiring interpersonal oral communication, such as the Mental Status Questionnaire.

A final consideration for management of speech-language impairments in the elderly has to do with prognosis and general focus.

First, it should be noted that almost all so-called "normative" data on speech function have been obtained on populations of much younger (often college-age) adults. Yet we have seen that the speech systems of the elderly vary sufficiently from those of younger adults as to make it unrealistic to use such data as benchmarks for estimation of severity and prognosis in the elderly. Second, it is self-defeating to place the major focus on deficits, or on what the individual cannot do. Rather, the focus should be mapping out all of the factors contributing to the individual's present level of communication function, on exploring and defining his/her maximum communication potential, and on assessing the differences between habitual performance and maximum potential. Whatever the individual's current status with respect to biologic aging and/or health status, and whatever the maximum communication potential may be, prognosis should be based on the probability of attaining that potential, given availability of appropriate services.

Therapeutic effectiveness for oral communication disorders involves much more than an interaction between the subject and the speech-language pathologist. Little will be gained unless attendance at individual therapy sessions is consistent, and unless therapeutic procedures are carried over into the individual's environment. This means that someone, the patient-client or a caregiver, must take responsibility for that consistent attendance, no small task either in an institution or in the community. It means that someone must be responsible for carry-over into the environment. This doesn't necessarily mean doing some sort of speech-language "exercises" with the subject. But it may mean that someone will have to pay attention to speech facilitating conditions, such as the subject's general body posture or the level of ambient noise. Or, it may mean that someone will have to become familiar with the use of a miniature amplifier for a subject with a very weak voice, or with a language board or electronic communication aid for the severely dysarthric. These are but a few of the possibilities. Whether we are dealing with speech-language disorders, reduced speech efficiency due to aging, or to inadequate communication environments, improved communication function rests on the cooperative efforts of the elderly individual, the speech-language clinician, and equally, on the efforts of other participants in the communicative situations.

It is our belief that all of these parties will find the effort worthwhile.

REFERENCES

Lubinski, R. Speech, language and audiology programs in home health care and nursing homes. In *Aging: Communication Processes and Disorders.* Beasley, D. and Davis, A. (Eds), New York: Grune and Stratton, 1981.

Lubinski, R. Why so little interest in whether or not old people talk: A review of recent research on verbal communication of the elderly. *International Journal of Aging and Human Development,* 9, 1979, 237-46.

The Environmental Role in Communication Skills and Opportunities of Older People

Rosemary Lubinski

A malignant tumor is one which destroys cells as it invades surrounding tissue. Gradually, the healthy tissue loses its identity to the encroaching mass. All networks of communication between the healthy cells are severed until they are isolated, degenerate, and finally die.

This description of malignancy portrays what happens to the elderly as they live in communication impaired environments such as long-term care institutions. Little by little the individual surrenders more personal identity to the institution, and simultaneously, the environment reduces or severs communication opportunities from the person. The result is a vicious circle: the aged person cannot exist without the long-term care institution, nor can this environment encourage growth and development for the older individual.

The first purpose of this paper is to describe the relationship of the environment to the communication skills and opportunities of older people, particularly those who live in nursing homes or other long-term care settings. The assumption underlying this discussion is that the environment is a crucial determinant in communication, and thus, can be a therapeutic agent in creating a positive communication atmosphere. The second purpose of the paper is to present some suggestions for the identification and remediation of com-

Rosemary Lubinski, PhD, is Associate Professor, Department of Communicative Disorders and Sciences, State University of New York at Buffalo. This paper was submitted following presentations given at "Aging and Communication: Problems and Management," sponsored by Teachers College, Columbia University, Brookdale Institute on Aging and Adult Human Development, October 16, 1981.

munication impaired environments in which older persons may live.*

ENVIRONMENT AND THE ELDERLY

Environment is defined as the external and internal forces which impinge upon a person throughout the life cycle. The external environment is composed of the physical surroundings and the socio-cultural climate. These create the background in which people function and help determine where they will live, how they will live, and the rules needed to maintain organization in that environment. The internal environment includes the spectrum of physical, intellectual, and affective traits each person contributes to the environment. In addition to these personal qualities, the individual brings a variety of needs, from those serving life maintenance to self-esteem. Ideally, there will be harmony when the person interacts with the physical and socio-cultural (external) environment. Sociologists call this adapting or integration.

The environment changes dramatically and often suddenly for many older people. The nature of the physical environment in which the older person lives and works is likely to change. For example, the older person may seek a smaller apartment with less maintenance responsibilities, move to a new locale, choose to live with family members, or relocate to a long-term care setting. In many cases, the person gives up possessions and reduces personal and private space. Further, retirement generally means withdrawal from long accustomed work areas associated with their jobs or professions.

Similarly, the socio-cultural determinants within the environment recast themselves. The older person must learn new rules for interacting within the environment. For example, the older person may need to learn how to live without a spouse, how to communicate

---

*It should be noted that this author has presented the material in this paper in several other works including Lubinski, R., Language and Aging: An environmental approach to intervention. *Topics in Language Disorders* 1981, 89-97; Lubinski, R., Perception of spoken communication by elderly chronically ill patients in an institutional setting. *Journal of Speech and Hearing Disorders* 1981, 46, 405-412. Lubinski, R., Speech, language and audiology programs in home health care and nursing homes. In *Aging: Communication Processes and Disorders*. Beasley, D. & Davis, A. (Eds.), New York: Grune & Stratton, 1981.

with adult children, and how to accept help as abilities change, perhaps diminish, and dependence increases.

Further, as persons age their own changes will have an influence on their environment. As physical abilities diminish adjustments are made in the environment so that the person can function adequately. Furniture may be arranged to facilitate mobility, and possessions may be given away or stored to ease mobility and cleaning. Strangers may come into the home to provide help with activities of daily living, thus becoming quasi-managers of that environment. In some cases when the individual becomes incapable of caring for his own needs, relocation to an institution may become the only alternative. Thus, the older person may relinquish independence, possessions, space and privacy, and symbols of personal identity as a trade off for shelter and care.

The older person's perception of the environmental changes are as important as the actual changes themselves. Perceived reality functions in tandem with objective reality in guiding behavior. For some older individuals, the perceived changes in themselves and their environment may differ substantially from what is actually occurring. One older individual may feel capable of independent living even when physical and/or cognitive abilities preclude this activity. Conversely, another elderly person may assume an attitude of learned-helplessness, defined as the perceived inability to surmount failure associated with such uncontrollable factors as aging and reduced abilities (Dweck, 1975; Diener and Dweck, 1978). Thus, the older person may be in conflict with the environment if there is over or underestimation of functional ability.

One of the most important consequences of environmental change for the elderly is the reduction in the range of options available. The modifications in the individual and the surroundings generally result in more controls, more limitations on behavior, and less personal choice (Proshansky, Ittleson, and Rivlin, 1976).

COMMUNICATION AND THE ELDERLY

Communication can be defined as the specific motor, cognitive, and sensory skills needed to send and receive messages: speech, language, and auditory and visual comprehension. People communicate through words and other nonverbal symbols such as gestures, signs, and movements. Communication is, however, more than a skill. Communication is the basic life experience. It allows us to receive information that will keep us alive and healthy. Good health and mental abilities are dependent upon a person listening, understanding, and talking about a variety of perceptions and ideas occurring in the environment. For the elderly the ability to communicate is crucial to life maintenance and personal satisfaction.

Through communication the elderly must obtain the information needed to live effectively in new or changing environments. For example, older individuals must be able to communicate with officials in government agencies and third party payment carriers in order to use Medicare benefits for health care. Older persons also learn the rules and expectations of their environment by listening and watching. It is common to find older persons in the community congregated in communal areas such as parks and shopping centers where they may observe the social changes occurring within their environment. Similarly, older persons in nursing homes cluster around the nurses' station and lobbies, again places where they might absorb the modus operandi of that setting.

It is also through communication that the older person maintains a sense of self identity and social connectedness to the social environment. Speech and language provide the vehicle for expressing inner thoughts which reflect social power and the need to influence others (Thibant and Kelley, 1959). Social theorists such as Mead (1934) and Erickson (1959) both stress the formation of self identity through interpersonal communication as a life long and evolving process. Through communication there are opportunities for reflecting upon the past and hypothesizing upon the future as a means of understanding one's identity in the present. Further, communication plays a therapeutic role by providing a means to vent anxiety, relieve loneliness, and resolve depression. The Bell Telephone jingle "Reach out, reach out and touch someone" is based on the concept that communication is the primary ingredient in both social connectedness and psychological well-being.

Finally, communication is the means by which older persons can negotiate with others in their environment. Patton and Griffin (1974) state that one of man's basic problems is "How can I maintain my own personal freedom and obtain your needed assistance in achieving my personal goals?'' (p. 113). Thus for the healthy older person communication may be the *crucial skill* in negotiating the right to remain independent. For those with more disabilities, it may be the skill most important to maintain through rehabilitation in order to prevent further deterioration, isolation, and dependence.

POSITIVE COMMUNICATION ENVIRONMENT

In order for older people to communicate successfully there must be two ingredients: first, there must be an external environment conducive to sending and receiving messages and second, the elderly need to retain the skills and motivation to communicate.

The physical environment should be designed to encourage opportunities to communicate with meaningful partners in a variety of activities. Physical access and mobility underlie opportunities to communicate, and hence, a physical environment which restricts mobility also restricts communication. Further, the older person with physical limitations may need special devices to promote communication or make it more efficient and effective. For example, easy access to a telephone and typewriter make communication possible with those outside the immediate setting. A special amplifier on the telephone makes calling a successful communication event for so many of the hearing impaired elderly. Alternate communication devices such as sentence construction boards, picture boards, and speech synthesizers aid the elderly who have severe communication problems.

Further, the sensory environment must be adequate for sending and receiving messages with maximum fidelity and minimum interference and distortion. For older persons who have vision and hearing problems, the quality of the sensory environment becomes important in communicating successfully. The sensory environment encompasses more than visual and auditory stimuli; however, all sensory avenues including taste, touch, and smell generate information which becomes a source of communication ideas and topics.

Successful communication is also dependent upon an accepting socio-cultural environment, one in which there is a reciprocal expression of trust. Thus, older individuals are likely to experience meaningful communication where there is a supportive social climate, free of evaluation and control and which enhances spontaneous expression, active listening, and constructive feedback.

Finally, the communication skills and motivation the older person contributes to each encounter play a role in its success. A stimulating and accepting environment is not sufficient. The older person must have some minimum ability to send, receive, and interpret messages. If these skills are reduced because of trauma, illness, or changes associated with aging, rehabilitation efforts are essential. Rehabilitation in the case of the elderly may not mean returning the skill to a previous normal level, but it may mean helping the individual to develop compensatory strategies and to use alternative communication devices. Rehabilitation may also entail counseling to help the person understand the changes in ability and opportunity to communicate. Communication disorders specialists, audiologists, and speech-language pathologists can provide diagnostic, therapy, and counseling services to older people and the significant people in their environment.

The older person must also be motivated to communicate. Research (Lubinski, 1979; Lubinski et al., 1981) indicates that elderly individuals in long-term care settings like to talk, want to talk, and feel it is important to their well being. Communication does not occur simply because people sit next to each other or live together. Communication erupts when older people are stimulated by interesting activities, when they are involved in situations which stimulate thinking and problem solving, and when they perceive that their contribution to a communicative event will be valued by others.

IDENTIFICATION OF THE COMMUNICATION IMPAIRED ENVIRONMENT

Goffman in his text *Asylums* (1961) outlined the conceptualization of a total environment. He defined a total institution as one which possesses psycho-social characteristics that make the setting all encompassing and restraining for the individuals within it. Bennett (1963) codified this totality theory into ten criteria which describe residential patterns and rules, philosophy of living, and personal freedoms available or not available in total institutions. An eleventh criterion might be added to Bennett's formula: the communication atmosphere of the environment. One aspect of an environment which contributes to its all encompassing and restraining nature is the degree of communication opportunity available there. While environments may range on a continuum with respect to communication opportunity, it is the negative end of the scale which is described as having specific deleterious effects on older individuals and is thus the subject of the remaining two sections of this paper. This is called a communication impaired environment.

A communication impaired environment is a setting in which there are few or limited opportunities for successful meaningful communication. Ten characteristics describe this environment.

1. There is a lack of sensitivity on the part of the significant persons in this environment to the value of interpersonal communication as a cornerstone of effective functioning and continuing self-realization. The significant others include administrators and staff of long-term care institutions, family, and others who interact with the elderly. In a communication impaired environment, communication is not perceived as a goal of the setting nor is its therapeutic effect realized. Communication between this older person and others is perceived as a by-product of the care given by staff or family.

2. There are rules which restrict the quantity and quality of communication among the persons living and interacting in that setting. There may be definite rules which prohibit talking at certain times or places or with specific people. In addition, there may be powerful covert rules which restrict communication in the same ways.

3. There is little reason to talk. Individuals in a communication impaired environment may participate in few activities which stimulate productive thinking and problem solving.

4. Similarly, the individuals in this setting perceive little value in communicating. Their ideas do not contribute to the decision making necessary to management of daily life. Thus, their communication becomes restricted to little more than the

social amenities used in interaction and the expression of basic personal needs.

5. In a communication impaired environment there are few persons perceived as viable communication partners. Some may be viewed with distrust and contempt, while others are never approached because of perceived negative characteristics such as race, ethnicity, presence of communication disabilities, and serious health and/or mental disorders.

6. There is a lack of privacy in which to have a conversation which is not under the scrutiny of others.

7. There is limited accessibility to others because of physical barriers or restraints on contacts. In a communication impaired environment individuals may not be able to come into a reasonable distance with others in order to send and receive verbal and nonverbal messages. Further, there may be limited access to devices which would amplify or enhance communication skills and opportunity such as hearing aids, acoustical treatment of walls and floors, or illumination control to provide the best possible use of hearing and vision.

8. There is a lack of sensory and cognitive stimulation. This is a setting which is devoid of creative activities and interesting sensory stimuli.

9. This is also an environment where there is little interaction with others outside the setting such as family, friends, and stimulating people.

10. Finally, in this environment suggestions for improving the communication atmosphere are met with resistance or rejection. For example, funds are not appropriated for inservice training of staff members or resident/patient suggestions are shelved indefinitely.

In order to determine the degree of communication impairment existing in environments in which older people live, these ten criteria can become sets of questions to be used in observing the communication atmosphere. While a standardized score is not availble to compare environments, the questions can serve as a basis for structured observation, yielding a profile of communication opportunities and barriers.

CREATING THE POSITIVE COMMUNICATION ENVIRONMENT

The question then becomes what can be done to improve the communication impaired environment and make it a positive communication atmosphere where communication opportunities are plentiful and rich. Suggestions form the framework for modifying environments which appear to be impaired.

First, *all* individuals in the environment must understand the importance of communication to the elderly and the negative effects of communication deprivation. This includes administrators, nursing/medical staff, housekeeping and dietary staff, other professionals, family, and the older person him/herself. A vehicle for informing these individuals is inservice or counseling. In both inservice to staff and counseling to the older individual and family, the goal is to develop an understanding of the value of communication to all persons involved. Not only is a positive communication environment a benefit for the aged but all others involved in this care. An environment where people communicate freely and openly is bound to be one where care givers work efficiently and effectively. Further, a positive communication atmosphere promotes family interaction with the older individual and follow-through on staff suggestions.

Second, the best suggestions for improving communication come from the people involved. Inservice and counseling do not mean telling the participants what to do in cook book fashion. The best suggestions are those which the participants generate themselves, which flow from their increased sensitivity to the communication opportunities and barriers in their environment. Learning theory states that discovery learning is powerful and is implemented thoughtfully.

Third, we need to become communication engineers, manipulators of the physical environment. Individuals who are interested in promoting a positive communication environment must first identify the physical restraints imposed on interaction in their setting. For example, acoustic treatment of walls and floors, window treatment to reduce glare, and improved accessibility all result in an environment conducive to exchanging verbal and nonverbal messages.

Fourth, these communication engineers must observe the quality of interaction which does occur in their setting: where do people talk, to whom, for what reasons, who is a communication leader. Sometimes simply knowing the background of the residents and then matching individuals with similar interests can promote communication.

Fifth, we must learn how to initiate and end conversations with older people. Rather than strive for clinical neutrality, staff members should share interesting parts of their lives as seeds for conversations. Further, staff must listen actively to the comments of older people, avoiding agreeing simply because that is the easy response. In addition, staff need to learn to monitor their nonverbal communication, that language transmitted through eye contact, facial expression, gesture, posture, and tone of voice.

Sixth, staff and family should encourage older persons to take advantage of speech and hearing professionals who can identify and provide therapy/intervention for any communication problems they may exhibit. Such disorders may be associated with stroke, senility, progressive neurological disease, cancer, or hearing loss.

Seventh, communication should be encouraged with individuals outside the environment. These persons may be lifelong friends or new acquaintances developed through participation in meaningful activities. Such programs as Adopt-a-Grandparent and volunteer services create new relationships for the older person.

Intervening in a communication impaired environment does not mean making everyone talk incessantly. The goal is successful and meaningful communication done in a supportive and encouraging atmosphere. The quality of an older person's communication skills and opportunities is an index of his social security.

REFERENCES

Bennett, R. The meaning of institutional life. *The Gerontologist,* 1963, 3, 117-24.
Diener, C. and Dweck, C. An analysis of learned helplessness: Continuous changes in performance, strategy and achievement cognitions following failure. *Journal of Social Psychology,* 36, 1978, 451-462.
Dweck, C. The role of expectations and attributions in the alleviation of learned helplessness. *Journal of Personality and Social Psychology,* 31, 1975, 674-685.
Erickson, E. The problem of ego identity. *Psychological Issues,* 1, 1959.
Goffman, E. *Asylums.* New York: Free Press, 1963.

Lubinski, R., Morrison, E., and Rigrodsky, S. Perception of spoken communication by elderly chronically ill patients in an institutional setting. *Journal of Speech and Hearing Disorders,* 1981.

Lubinski, R. Speech, language and audiology programs in home health care and nursing homes. In *Aging: Communication Processes and Disorders.* Beasley, D. and Davis, G. A. (Eds.), New York: Grune & Stratton, 1981.

Lubinski, R. Why so little interest in whether or not old people talk: A review of recent research on verbal communication of the elderly. *International Journal of Aging and Human Development,* 9, 1979, 237-46.

Mead, G. *Mind, Self and Society.* Chicago: University of Chicago Press, 1934.

Patton, B. and Giffin, K. *Interpersonal Communication.* New York: Harper and Row, 1974.

Proshansky, H., Ittleson, W., and Rivlin, L. *Environmental Psychology.* New York: Holt, Rinehart and Winston, 1976.

Thibant, J. and Kelley, H. *The Social Psychology of Groups.* New York: Wiley, 1959.

Legislation Affecting the Delivery of Speech-Language-Hearing Services to the Elderly

Barbara E. Weinstein

The provision of speech-language pathology and audiology services to the communicatively impaired elderly has recently become a major public policy issue as evidenced by the legislation authorizing health insurance programs and specific services for the elderly. A thorough understanding of the government policies underlying the provision of speech-language pathology and audiology services is an integral part of the health care delivery system to the elderly. It is hoped that a brief overview of the government's role in the provision of speech-language and hearing services will facilitate more informed decisions on the part of the elderly.

Third-Party Payment for Hearing Aids

Medicare and Medicaid are the major federal/state health insurance programs which help to defray the costs associated with speech and hearing services. Medicare is a federally operated health insurance program for individuals over 65 years of age, while Medicaid is the medical assistance program designed to serve the needy and medically indigent. A small number of individuals 65 and older benefit from both programs (American Speech-Language and Hearing Association, 1980).

Barbara E. Weinstein, PhD, is Assistant Professor in the Department of Speech-Language Pathology and Audiology, Teachers College, Columbia University.

In the interest of clarity, speech-language pathology and audiology services under Medicare and Medicaid will be outlined separately.*

MEDICARE

Speech and hearing services are reimbursable under Medicare provided the following conditions are met:

a. the facility is certified to provide Medicare services.
b. the speech pathologist or audiologist is a qualified provider (i.e., the professional holds a Certificate of Clinical Competence in the appropriate area or a valid state license).
c. the patient is an eligible Medicare beneficiary.

Speech-Language Pathology Under Medicare

Prior to discussing the benefits under Medicare, the three conditions which must be met for reimbursement are as follows:

1. A physician must refer the patient to a *qualified* speech pathologist for speech-language pathology services. The therapy must be rendered under a plan of treatment prescribed by a physician *or* speech pathologist. A physician must recertify the need for continued treatment on a regular basis.
2. The therapeutic intervention must be related to the condition for which the patient was hospitalized, and must be necessary to the treatment of the condition.
3. There must be a reasonable expectation for progress and restoration of speech/language function if the services are to be reimbursed (ASHA, 1981).

Under Part A of Medicare (i.e., hospital insurance) speech-language pathology services are available to hospital inpatients, to

---

*The information on legislation is based on information contained in the federal register (1977), the ASHA Government Affairs Review, and the chapter by Dowling (1981) in the text titled *Aging: Communication Processes and Disorders.*

patients in skilled nursing facilities (SNF), and as a health benefit to homebound patients receiving home health services (Dowling, 1981). Speech-language pathology services may be rendered by a speech-language pathologist who is a hospital employee or has a contractual arrangement with the hospital. When speech-language pathology services are offered as an extended care benefit to residents in a skilled nursing facility, the service can be rendered by an SNF employee or by a speech pathologist who has a contractual arrangement with the SNF (ASHA, 1980). A separate nursing facility-hospital agreement is required if a speech pathologist employed by the transferring hospital provides the services (Dowling, 1981). With respect to home health benefits, services are available to the homebound provided the treatment is for the condition for which the patient was hospitalized. Dollar guidelines for service reimbursement are developed on an annual basis and are published regularly in the Federal Register. One final point: as of July 1981, there is no limit on the number of home health visits to which an individual is entitled (ASHA, 1981).

Under Part B of Medicare (medical insurance), outpatient speech pathology services may be provided in a hospital, outpatient speech and hearing clinic, or in a rehabilitation agency. It must be emphasized that Medicare *will not* reimburse a private practitioner directly. Rather, speech-language pathologists are reimbursed by the facility with which he/she has a contractual arrangement. In the latter case, the facility will be reimbursed for the service and in turn will pay the private practitioner. Finally, Part B also provides for unlimited home health visits for eligible Medicare beneficiaries (ASHA, 1981).

Audiology Under Medicare

Audiologic services can be covered under Medicare; however, the range of reimbursable services is limited. Under Part A, diagnostic and therapeutic audiologic services requested by a physician and rendered in a hospital are reimbursable. Specifically, the only diagnostic services which are covered are those requested by a physician to assist in a medical diagnosis. Similarly, therapeutic services are covered when provided to hospital inpatients for the condition for which the beneficiary is hospitalized (ASHA, 1980). The audiologist must be an employee of the hospital or have a contractual arrangement with the hospital to receive reimbursement for services. If the hospital in which the audiologist is employed and the SNF have a separate transfer agreement, audiological services for patients transferred to an SNF will be covered. Part B of Medicare also provides coverage for diagnostic audiology services, provided a physician requests the evaluation to assist in a medical diagnosis. Thus, covered audiological services must be requested by a physician. Medicare *will not* reimburse for hearing evaluations performed for the purpose of determining the need for a hearing aid nor for the selection of hearing aids. Similarly, Medicare *will not* cover therapeutic audiological services rendered in the office of a private practitioner, nor will it reimburse for a hearing aid. It is of interest that diagnostic and therapeutic services may be provided as a Part B benefit by an audiologist employed by a physician or in a physician-directed clinic, provided the service is an integral part of the physician's professional services. Finally, it should be noted that in contrast to speech pathology services, an audiologist in private practice, with a Medicare provider number, can be directly reimbursed by Medicare.

Speech-language pathologists and audiologists are currently working toward expanding speech pathology and audiology benefits. For example, efforts are being directed toward reimbursement for speech-language pathology services provided in the office of a private practitioner. Additionally, elderly consumer groups are advocating coverage for the cost of hearing aids; as on their meager social security payments, senior citizens can hardly afford to purchase a hearing aid (Dowling, 1981; ASHA, 1981).

MEDICAID

Speech-Language Pathology Under Medicaid

Unlike Medicare, Medicaid has few national requirements. In addition to setting eligibility requirements, each state decides on the medical and rehabilitative services to be provided to the financially needy. As such, there are substantial state to state variations in the type and extent of services. States are constantly increasing or decreasing their benefit programs. At present, inflation and "Reagan-omics" have led to more coverage reductions than increases (Dow-ling, 1981).

States may include up to 17 different categories of services into their Medicaid program. Five services are mandatory and the re-mainder optional. Speech and hearing services ordinarily provided to inpatients in the hospital must be reimbursed by all state Medicaid programs. Similarly, speech pathology/audiology services must be provided as needed by SNF's participating in Medicaid; of course, each facility must be Medicaid approved if the institution is to be re-imbursed for its services (ASHA, 1981). Given the substantial state to state variations, it is beyond the scope of this paper to discuss the structure of individual state programs. Dowling (1981) suggests that direct contact with the agency administering the program will allow one to learn the specifics of a given Medicaid program. To illustrate the structure of Medicaid programs, I will describe briefly New York State's Medicaid Program as of Fall 1981.

In New York State, Medicaid will reimburse for speech pathol-ogy services when provided by an approved home health agency. In addition, Medicaid will reimburse a speech pathologist involved in private practice for services rendered, provided he/she has a Medicaid provider number and a physician authorizes and regularly recertifies the need for therapy. In addition, prior approval from the medical director at the state Medicaid office is required. With re-spect to audiological services, Medicaid will reimburse for hearing aids as long as the supplier has a provider number. Dispensing aud-iologists and hearing aid dealers can, therefore, be reimbursed for the sale of hearing aids. An individual must be evaluated by an ear specialist and receive an audiological evaluation for reimbursement for a hearing aid. It should be noted that Medicaid sets a limit on the dollar amount for reimbursement and the amounts are adjusted on a regular basis. The price will depend upon the type of fitting (mon-aural vs. binaural) as well as the type of hearing aid (e.g., body aid vs. in-the-ear aid). In addition, one can be reimbursed for hearing aid batteries, replacement parts, earmolds, and repairs. Again, the latter items must be purchased from a supplier with a Medicaid pro-vider number. Finally, Medicaid will reimburse approved facilities for audiological and hearing aid evaluations; however, audiologists in private practice are not eligible. To reiterate, the above conditions for reimbursement apply to New York State. Each state agency issues its own guidelines for reimbursement. This information is available from the state Medicaid office.

As is evident from the brief overview of federal health insurance programs, Medicare and Medicaid reimbursement is limited, and the probability of expanding services is minimal. Private insurance agencies have increased the accessibility of services for the communicatively handicapped. Although health insurance policies rarely provide for explicit coverage of speech-language pathology and audiology services, they will cover certain services under the guise of "miscellaneous medical" or "medically necessary services" (ASHA, 1981). Unfortunately, the conditions and practices governing private insurance providers vary, and space does not permit a lengthy discussion of the services which are reimbursed by each insurance company. In general, major medical policies such as Prudential and Aetna will cover speech-language pathology services provided to help regain speech or language function lost due to illness. Similarly, audiometric testing required to establish a diagnosis is often covered. The majority of policies exclude hearing aid evaluations and hearing aids, however, recently insurance companies have been expanding their services to include reimbursement and hearing aids. To facilitate the reimbursement process, one must scrutinize the insurance policy to determine the conditions under which speech-language pathology and audiology services are rendered and complete the forms accordingly (ASHA, 1980).

One additional source of financial support for the communicatively impaired older adult is the Veterans Administration (VA). For example, the VA will provide assistance in acquiring audiological evaluations and hearing aids to certain groups of veterans. The conditions under which services can be obtained should be explored on an individual basis at a local Veterans Administration Medical Center.

Federal Regulations Governing Hearing Aid Delivery

The federal government has recently acknowledged that the older adult tends to be vulnerable to "sales abuse, misevaluations and misrepresentations" (FDA, 1977). Accordingly, the Food and Drug

Administration (FDA), an independent agency within the Health and Human Services Department, has promulgated national standards for the provision of hearing aids to the hearing impaired. The intent of the FDA regulations is to protect the health and safety of the hearing impaired consumer (FDA, 1977).

The restrictions imposed by the FDA relate to labeling, instructional, and warning statements, and to conditions for sale (FDA, 1977). Specifically, the FDA requires a medical examination by a licensed physician within six months preceding the sale of the hearing aid to insure that the particular hearing loss is not amenable to medical or surgical intervention. The physician must furnish the prospective hearing aid user with a written statement indicating that the patient may be considered a candidate for a hearing aid. Although not in the patient's best interest, an individual over 18 years of age may waive the requirement for medical clearance. However, hearing aid dispensers are prohibited from encouraging the client to exercise the waiver. The adult client wishing to waive the medical evaluation must be informed that such an action is not in his/her best interest. Although an audiological evaluation is strongly recommended, it is not required by the FDA (FDA, 1977). An additional condition for sale is that an instructional brochure containing technical data, a description of the controls, as well as a discussion of hearing aid maintenance must accompany each hearing aid. The contents of the user's instructional brochure must be reviewed with the consumer prior to the sale. Finally, the FDA regulations recommend that the consumer inquire about the possibility of a trial rental or purchase option program. Most hearing aid dealers allow the prospective wearer a trial period of thirty days before making a final decision about purchasing a hearing aid. New York State requires that a 30-day money back written guarantee accompany all hearing aid sales. The consumer is, thus, entitled to return the hearing aid within thirty days, and receive the purchase price minus a small cancellation fee (FDA, 1977).

Unfortunately, time does not permit a more extensive discussion of the federal and state regulations governing the delivery of speech and hearing services. It is hoped that the brief overview will enable health care professionals to assist the elderly consumer to make more informed decisions. Additional information about legislation governing speech-language and audiological services is available from the American Speech-Language-Hearing Association.

REFERENCES

American Speech-Language and Hearing Association. A report on third party reimbursement of speech-language pathology and audiology services. *Governmental Affairs Review,* 1980.

American Speech-Language and Hearing Association. *Governmental Affairs Review*—Medicare supplement, 1981.

Dowling, R. Federal health insurance for the elderly. In Beasley, D., Davis, G. (Eds.), *Aging: Communication Processes and Disorders.* New York: Grune and Stratton, 1981.

Food and Drug Administration. Hearing aid devices—professional and patient labeling and conditions for sale. Federal Register, *42,* (Feb. 15), 9286-9296, 1977.

Medicare Act of 1965, U.S.C. 42, 7, 1976.

Providing Services
to the Communicatively Impaired Elderly

Ira M. Ventry

The purpose of this presentation is to present an overview of the personnel and facilities available to provide services to the communicatively impaired. In essence, the question is: "Who can provide services and where and how can the services be provided?"

PERSONNEL

In terms of personnel, it should be obvious that services to the communicatively impaired should be provided by specialists in communication disorders—namely, speech and language pathologists and audiologists. Speech and language pathologists and audiologists are individuals who have either master's or doctoral degrees in speech and hearing and are qualified, by virtue of training and experience, to provide both diagnostic and treatment services to individuals with speech and hearing problems. I should emphasize that licensed and/or certified speech and language pathologists and audiologists are independent professionals who often work with, but *not* under, the *professional* supervision of other health personnel. Under certain conditions, a treatment plan may be required from a physician. The implementation of that plan, however, is the responsibility of the speech and language pathologist or audiologist. If, under certain circumstances, professional supervision is required, that supervision is provided by more qualified, more experienced speech and language pathologists and audiologists.

Most speech and hearing professionals are members of at least

Ira M. Ventry, PhD, was Professor, Department of Speech and Language Pathology and Audiology, Teachers College, Columbia University.

two organizations—the American Speech-Language-Hearing Association (commonly known as ASHA) which is their national professional association—and their state (and sometimes their city) professional association. The reason I mention this is that ASHA's Certificate of Clinical Competence (or CCC) indicates that an individual has met certain minimal requirements with respect to academic training and clinical experience (in addition to passing a national examination) and is deemed competent by ASHA to provide diagnostic and treatment services to people with speech, hearing, and language problems. Therefore, one important way to determine if a person is qualified to provide services is to determine if they hold the CCC.

Perhaps a more important way to assess a person's qualifications is to determine if he or she holds a state license to practice speech/language pathology or audiology. We have licensure here in New York State; New Jersey does not. In New York State, the requirements for a license have been modeled on and are very similar to the certification requirements spelled out by ASHA. While people working in certain environments are exempt from licensing (for example, speech pathologists working in the schools or audiologists working in a Veterans Administration facility), there is no question but that private practitioners (for example, those people employed on a part-time or consultative basis in a nursing home) must be licensed by New York State. Federal and state and local regulations may also require that services be rendered by licensed practitioners.

To sum up, elderly people with communication problems will require the diagnostic and treatment services of qualified speech and language pathologists and audiologists. The qualifications of such people can be evaluated by determining if they hold the CCC and/or license in their respective specialties. In some settings, individuals *must* be *licensed* to practice. If I were to seek the services of a speech pathologist or audiologist to work with my elderly clients, I would look for one additional qualification. They should have had both academic preparation and clinical experience with older people. As we have heard, the elderly often present unique and difficult problems and these problems are most likely to be solved by professionals who come with appropriate training and experience in geriatric communicology.

Before I leave personnel, I should comment briefly about hearing aid dispensers. I mention this specifically because so many older people need and can benefit from hearing aids and because the hearing aid dispenser can be a very important part of the total aural rehabilitation program.

There are basically two kinds of people who dispense hearing aids. The first is an audiologist who is in private practice. This person, then, is a licensed audiologist as well as a registered hearing aid dealer or dispenser. In addition to selling or dispensing hearing aids, the audiologist in private practice offers a broad range of diagnostic and treatment services to hearing-impaired people. This is important because the hearing aid must be seen in the context of a total rehabilitation or treatment program.

The second kind of person who dispenses hearing aids is the hearing aid dealer. Hearing aid dealers, at least in New York State, are not licensed, may or may not have more than a high school education, may or may not be members of a national hearing aid society, may or may not have had specific training in audiology, and so on. As a result, the non-audiologist hearing aid dispenser is not equipped or licensed to provide the audiologic diagnostic and treatment or rehabilitative services so frequently required by the hearing-impaired elderly. They are well-versed, however, in the art of fitting and selling hearing aids. In my opinion, therefore, no elderly hearing-impaired person should purchase a hearing aid without having had a prior audiological evaluation to determine the person's need for an aid, their candidacy for a hearing aid, and to determine the need for a total rehabilitation program to insure successful use of amplification. In all fairness, I should point out that this opinion is not shared by non-audiologist hearing aid dispensers or by the U.S. Food and Drug Administration.

FACILITIES AND SETTINGS

Speech and language pathologists and audiologists can be found in a variety of settings ranging from the schools to industry, from rehabilitation centers to physicians' offices. For our purposes today, however, it would probably be best to focus on the speech and hearing center.

Speech and hearing centers, at least in the New York metropolitan area, are usually located in hospital settings and in colleges and universities. Nearly every major hospital in New York City has a speech and hearing center staffed by speech and language pathologists and audiologists. Oftentimes speech and hearing centers have on staff other professionals as well—social workers, otolaryngologists, psychologists, pediatricians, and the like. The typical hospital speech and hearing center is designed then to provide a full range of diagnostic and treatment services to communicatively impaired elderly people. The speech and hearing center is equipped to meet the needs of the laryngectomized, the aphasic adult, the hearing-impaired elderly and so on.

Just as there are professional standards which must be met by individual audiologists and speech and language pathologists, so too are there standards that speech and hearing centers should or must meet. ASHA not only certifies individuals but it also certifies, through a specific registration program, speech and hearing centers. That is, ASHA has promulgated a set of minimum standards and registers service programs that meet these standards. The standards cover such items as personnel, facilities, equipment, record keeping, and so on. ASHA's stamp of approval, in the form of registration, is one way of knowing that a service program has met national standards for the provision of speech and hearing services. It's a step in helping to insure quality service.

In New York City, there is another standard setting body (there is one at the state level as well) and that is the Department of Health's Bureau for Handicapped Children, known as BHC. Although designed to insure quality services for children, the BHC standards are such that they help insure quality services for all clients seen at BHC-approved speech and hearing centers. In fact, the standards set by the BHC are, on certain points, more rigorous than those promulgated by ASHA. There are approximately 22 speech and hearing centers approved by BHC, most of them located in large hospitals such as Bellevue, Columbia Presbyterian, Mt. Sinai, and Harlem Hospital.

In addition to speech and hearing centers located in hospital facilities, one can also find such centers within colleges and universities. We have such a center here at Teachers College and there are similar centers at Hunter College, Queens College, Brooklyn College, and so forth. Again, these centers usually provide a broad spectrum of speech and hearing services to individuals with communication disorders but the total range of services may be somewhat limited compared to those found in a hospital setting. For example, it would be an atypical university center that had easy access to a social worker. In addition to providing services to clients, centers located in university settings are frequently involved in student training. It should be emphasized that if a university program is approved by ASHA—and many are—then student training must not interfere with or serve as an obstacle to the provision of diagnostic and treatment services. ASHA makes that very clear.

Finally, there are freestanding operations that are not located in institutional settings but that provide a variety of services to the elderly. Perhaps the best example of such a program is the New York League for the Hard of Hearing. This is a non-profit community hearing center (it is approved by both ASHA and BHC) that provides a variety of services to hearing-impaired elderly. Unlike most speech and hearing centers that I have discussed, the League dispenses hearing aids as part of their total rehabilitation program. It is a major community resource and one of the largest of its kind in the world. I am unaware of a comparable or analogous facility in the speech and language area.

The point of all of this is to emphasize to you the breadth and depth of speech and hearing services available in the New York metropolitan area to elderly people with communication problems. The speech and hearing centers, the private practitioners, the college and university programs, the freestanding clinics are all available to you and to your clients. There are directories of services and listings of programs and individuals available from ASHA, from the New York State Department of Education, from the New York State Speech and Hearing Association. *Any* professional speech and language pathologist can also serve as a resource person to help you find programs and/or people to provide services for your clients. In my mind, there simply is not any good reason—and financial eligibility or third party reimbursements are not necessarily good reasons—for an elderly person with a communication disorder *not* to receive the services they need or deserve. The resources are available and all of us must do whatever we can to see to it that the resources are used by the people who require them.

THE NURSING HOME SETTING

The discussion about providing services would be incomplete without some attention devoted to the provision of services in long-term care facilities. In this case, of course, speech and hearing people usually come to the facility and to the client rather than the client going to the speech and hearing center—which is the case with community-based elderly.

As has been noted previously, the prevalence of communication problems among nursing home patients is much higher than that found among community-based elderly. We have also noted that elderly people living in the community have a variety of resources available to them. What are the resources available to patients in long-term care facilities and are the communication needs of these patients being met?

A recent article by Mueller and Peters (1981) addresses these questions for the State of Wisconsin. I would like to present their results in some detail because I think their data for Wisconsin can probably be generalized, albeit somewhat cautiously, to New York City and environs.

Figure 1 shows the distribution of communication disorders among 158 patients in a nursing home (the type of facility was not identified by the authors). Note that 60% had identifiable disorders of communication. It is important to point out that their 9% figure for hearing impairment is probably a gross underestimate of the numbers of patients with significant hearing impairment since their percentage is based on interview data, not on hearing test results. Mueller and Peters concluded that only about 50% of those identified could benefit from therapeutic intervention. Projecting their figures to the potential nursing home population in Wisconsin, Mueller and Peters estimated that more than 15,000 elderly adults could benefit from professional intervention.

Figure 2 shows that 85% of Wisconsin's speech and language pathologists and audiologists are *not* involved in providing services

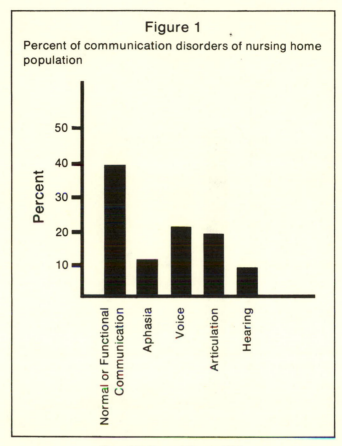

From Mueller and Peters, 1981.

to nursing home patients; only 9 professionals (2.5%) were directly employed by a long-term care facility.

Figures 3A and 3B are based on data supplied by nursing home administrators (N = 308). Note that administrators estimated that 20% of their residents had speech and language problems and that 34% had hearing problems. This latter figure is almost four times greater than that found by Mueller and Peters in their evaluation of nursing home residents while the speech and language estimates of the administrators is approximately half of that found by the authors.

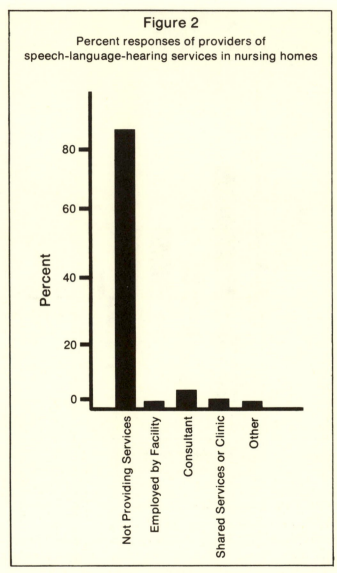

From Mueller and Peters, 1981.

Figures 4A and 4B simply confirm the earlier finding, namely that exceedingly few speech and hearing professionals are employed on either a part-time or full-time basis by nursing homes. It is interesting to note that the vast majority of nursing home administrators indicated that they had no plans to hire speech and hearing professionals in the future.

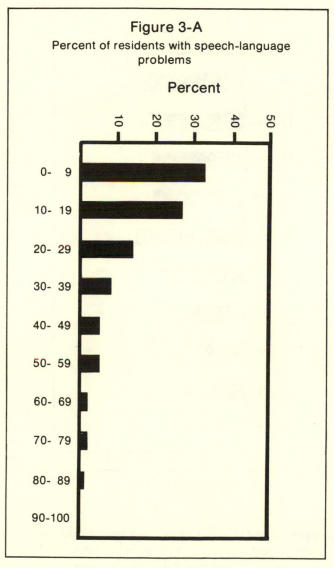

From Mueller and Peters, 1981.

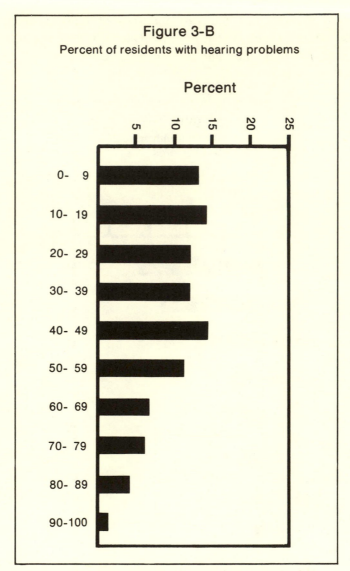

Figure 3-B

Percent of residents with hearing problems

From Mueller and Peters, 1981.

It is apparent from Figure 5 that most speech and hearing services in long-term care facilities in Wisconsin are provided by an outside agency or individual, and that the most common practice is the use of an "outside agency providing rehabilitation services on a contractual basis." The next most common means of providing services is through the use of a private practitioner.

As I am sure you recognize, the full scope of services that are provided (or not provided, as may be the case) cannot really be assessed from the data presented in Figure 5. As Mueller and Peters put it: "Since no data as to the quantity of these services were gathered in the survey, it is impossible to draw conclusions regarding the effectiveness or completeness of the aforementioned services." From my experience and information, I would dare say that most elderly people in institutional settings are not receiving adequate services. It is simply not adequate, for example, to employ a speech pathologist or audiologist several hours a week and expect that person to provide comprehensive services to the approximately 50% of the residents who need and can benefit from such services!

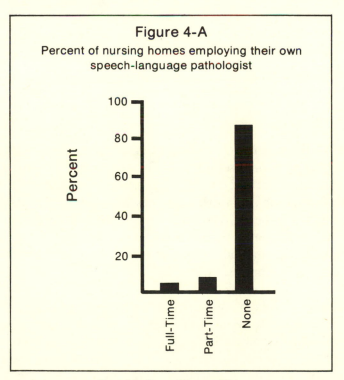

Figure 4-A

Percent of nursing homes employing their own speech-language pathologist

From Mueller and Peters, 1981.

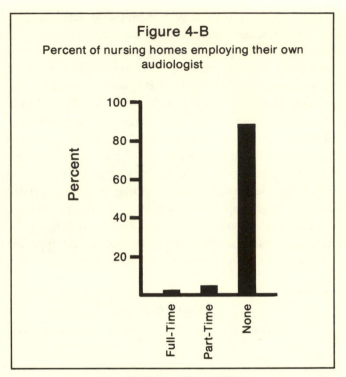

Figure 4-B

Percent of nursing homes employing their own audiologist

From Mueller and Peters, 1981.

The last figure (Figure 6) is interesting in that it identifies the reasons for not providing services. While the number of respondents was rather small here (N = 58), it is striking that nearly 40% indicated that speech and hearing services were not needed. And this is double the number of respondents who cited budgeting restraints as the reason for not providing services.

I am in agreement with the major conclusion drawn by Mueller and Peters. This conclusion is as follows:

> A large population of older adults who reside in extended care facilities are in need of the services of speech and language pathologists and audiologists. This need is being met inadequately or not at all. Nursing home administrators and other responsible parties should be urged to recognize the unmet

communication needs of their clients which can and should be managed professionally.

Before I conclude this part, let me describe briefly the kinds of services that can and should be provided by an audiologist working in a long-term care facility. I emphasize audiology here because I am most familiar with what audiologists can do and because audiologists are even less frequently employed in nursing home settings than speech and language pathologists. Similar services, of

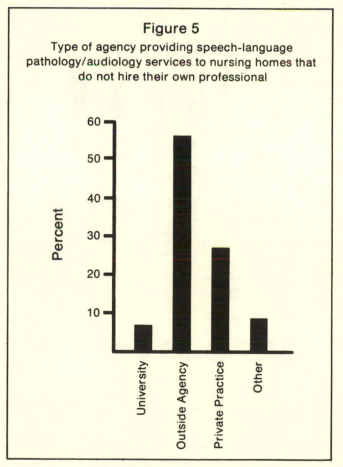

Figure 5

Type of agency providing speech-language pathology/audiology services to nursing homes that do not hire their own professional

From Mueller and Peters, 1981.

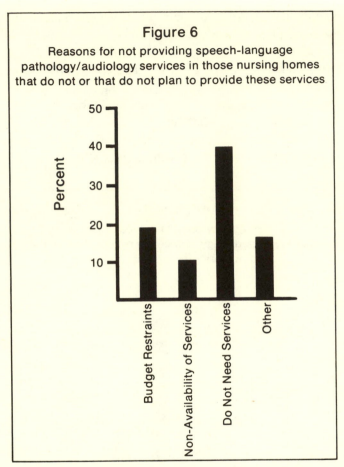

Figure 6

Reasons for not providing speech-language pathology/audiology services in those nursing homes that do not or that do not plan to provide these services

From Mueller and Peters, 1981.

course, can be provided by the speech-language pathologist. Here is the list of audiologic services:

1. Identification of people with hearing impairment;
2. Diagnosis and evaluation of the nature and extent of the hearing impairment;
3. Hearing aid selection and maintenance;
4. Hearing therapy including speechreading and auditory training;

5. Patient counseling and counseling of family members;
6. Inservice education;
7. Interaction with important community resources regarding follow-up services for individuals returning to the community;
8. Help facilitate a positive communication environment within the facility;
9. Serve as a resource person for staff and administration;
10. Evaluate the success and value of facility's audiology program.

There are probably other services that can be provided that I have not mentioned. The point is that total audiologic care should be the goal we strive toward and that this goal can best be achieved through the use of knowledgeable and dedicated clinicians who have the strong and unwavering support of knowledgeable and dedicated administrators.

HOME HEALTH CARE AGENCIES

I want to say just a few words about speech and hearing services provided to the elderly through home health care agencies. I should note that the discussion focuses on speech and language services because audiology services through home health care agencies are just about nonexistent!

Home health care services are provided in a number of different ways and by different agencies, for example, Visiting Nurses Associations. Two separate surveys indicate that approximately 50% of the home health care agencies provide speech and language services (5% in audiology) and most of the recipients of such services are 65 years of age or older. As might be expected, therefore, patients with aphasia/apraxia constitute the bulk of the speech clinician's caseload. Also as might be expected, the vast majority of agencies (89%) employ part-time speech pathologists—very few agencies hire full-time people. Somewhat disheartening is Lubinski and Chapey's (1980) finding that only 7% of the agencies surveyed indicated that they planned to improve speech and language services to the home-bound! A number of factors serve as obstacles to the provision of speech and hearing services as part of a home care program. Lubinski and Chapey identified 10 such factors, the most important of which were: the distance needed to travel to provide services; the availability of personnel (part-time people may not be available during the day); lack of family involvement; funding for services; and lack of physician referrals. Hester (1981) made the following suggestions for increasing speech and language services in home care programs:

1. State Medicaid agencies should allow for reimbursement of speech and language services in the home;
2. Private insurance companies should expand their coverage for such services;
3. Inservice training should be provided to other health professionals to increase their awareness of communication disorders;
4. Speech and language evaluations should be performed routinely on all CVA patients; and
5. Public education campaigns should alert people about the availability of speech and language services for home delivery.

In summary, although there seems a growing awareness of the need and value of home care speech and language services, much remains to be done to increase and upgrade these services. As Lubinski and Chapey (1980) stated: "Continued and improved communication effectiveness may well be a concrete skill which will contribute to social interaction and forestall isolation, institutionalization, or even death. Speech and hearing programs through home health care appear to be a realistic avenue for reaching the home-bound elderly" (p. 934).

CONCLUSIONS

There is little question but that speech, language, and hearing problems constitute a major handicap for many elderly people. There is little question but that many speech pathologists and audiologists are qualified by virtue of their training and experience to provide much needed services to our communicatively impaired elderly. There is little question but that many of our communicatively handicapped are *not* receiving the services that they need or that they may be entitled to. A major purpose of today's conference is to help you to help us bridge the gap between need and service. The gap must not get wider—perhaps our efforts today will insure that at least here in the metropolitan area, the gap will grow smaller and smaller until one day, the need for a conference such as the one today will no longer exist. Thank you.

CLOSING REMARKS

This monograph is not intended as a comprehensive review of "aging and communication." The thrust is twofold: to spur interest in understanding the complex relationship between the processes of aging and communication and to provide some practical help for caregivers. It is hoped that our efforts will be a first step toward facilitating communication with the elderly.

REFERENCES

Hester, E.J. The status of speech-language pathology in home health settings. *Asha,* 23, 1981, 155-161.

Lubinski, R., and Chapey, R. Communication services in home health agencies: Availability and scope. *Asha,* 22, 1981, 929-934.

Mueller, P., and Peters, T. Needs and services in geriatric speech-language pathology and audiology. *Asha,* 23, 1981, 627-632.